"Virtually every wedding and funeral scenario possible is covered, including legal issues in both U.S. and Canadian contexts. The book lives up to its title as a pastor's guide and will be welcomed by beginning and seasoned pastors alike."

—CBA Marketplace

THE PASTOR'S GUIDE TO

Weddings

&

Funerals

THE PASTOR'S GUIDE TO

Weddings

&

Funerals

VICTOR D. LEHMAN

Judson Press
Valley Forge

The Pastor's Guide to Weddings and Funerals
© 2001 by Judson Press, Valley Forge, PA 19482-0851
All rights reserved.

Unless otherwise indicated, Bible quotations in this volume are from the New
American Standard Bible, © 1960, 1962, 1963, 1968, 1971, 1972, 1973, 1975,
1977 by The Lockman Foundation. Used by permission.

Scriptures designated KJV are from *The Holy Bible, King James Version*. Bible
quotations designated TLB are from *The Living Bible,* copyright © 1971. Used by permission of Tyndale House Publishers, Inc., Wheaton, IL 60189. All rights reserved.
Scriptures designated THE MESSAGE are from *THE MESSAGE*. Copyright © by Eugene
H. Peterson 1993, 1994, 1995. Used by permission of NavPress Publishing Group.
Scriptures designated NRSV are from the *New Revised Standard Version of the Bible,*
copyright 1989 by the Division of Christian Education of the National Council of the
Churches of Christ in the USA. Used by permission. Scriptures designated NIV are
from *HOLY BIBLE: New International Version,* copyright © 1973, 1978, 1984.
Used by permission of Zondervan Bible Publishers. Scriptures designated *The New
Translation* are from Kenneth Taylor, ed., *The New Translation: The Letters of the
New Testament,* Tyndale House Publishers, Inc., 1990.

Library of Congress Cataloging-in-Publication Data
Lehman, Victor D.
    The pastor's guide to weddings and funerals / Victor D. Lehman.
        p. cm.
    Includes bibliographical references.
    ISBN 0-8170-1392-X (pbk. : alk. paper)
    1. Marriage service. 2. Funeral service. 3. Pastoral theology. I. Title.

BV199.M3 L44 2001
265'.5—dc21   00-067528

Printed in the U.S.A.
07 06 05
10 9 8 7 6 5 4

*T*his book is dedicated

to beginning pastors,

in Canada and the United States,

who are struggling with

the many "firsts" of ministry.

May this resource manual serve as your mentor,

coaching you through the sensitive preparation

of exceptional weddings and funerals.

Contents

CONTENTS

CONTENTS

Part II: Funerals

CONTENTS

6: Funeral Service Resources

CONTENTS

Appendixes: Additional Wedding and Funeral Resources

Preface

The young minister was in a quandary. Something about this particular couple desiring to marry just did not feel right. They appeared to love each other. At least they made an effort to show this affection when in the pastor's study for premarital counseling. But something did not appear genuine. Perhaps it was the isolated way in which they walked to their separate cars after each counseling session, thinking themselves unseen. During these partings, they never touched each other. Instead, they appeared to have dropped a pretense and begun acting businesslike, similar to clients arranging a contract. Perhaps this behavior was normal in their culture. Perhaps everything about their relationship was authentic. But why did the minister have this foreboding sense of simply being used to formalize and bless a merely legal agreement?

"Oh, Pastor," the grief-stricken widow gushed, "thank you so much for all your support during these last three days. I don't know how I would have survived without you!" As she turned to leave the pastor's study and join the rest of the family for the funeral, she paused at the doorway. "If you could just do one more thing for me, I would be so appreciative. I know my husband was not a very religious man, and maybe some of his business practices were a little questionable, but could you make him 'look good' in this funeral service? We do need to respect the dead, do we not?"

PRETENSE, OPEN DECEIT, strong expectations, and unfair pressure all regularly arrive at the pastor's door. Each incident challenges a pastor's ethical standards and integrity. Experience tends to equip us to make better decisions in questionable circumstances. But what of the pastor who is just beginning ministry? Who will help him or her when the mentors of seminary are now too far away?

This field manual is written to help stand in that gap. It combines the author's ten years of personal pastoral experience with the experiences of ministerial colleagues in an effort to put seasoned experience at the fingertips of ministers struggling with all the challenging "firsts" of ministry.

This manual is intended to be a "hands-on" resource. It provides ethical guidance for conducting challenging weddings and funerals, helpful checklists as to what elements are used in a typical wedding or funeral, and practical resources, such as appropriate Scriptures, sermon outlines, and wedding vows. These resources also can be downloaded from the Judson Press website at www.judsonpress.com. Simply click on the "Free Downloads" starburst on the upper right of your screen. Under the "Special Offers" section at the upper left, enter the password PAGUWE0450 in the box and click "Go." You should see an image of the book cover and below it is a list of the material that is available online. You have the option of choosing to preview or download each item. Choose the information you need, download or copy and paste it to your computer's hard drive, and then revise it as needed to fit your situation before printing out a copy for reference during the actual service or ceremony.

If you need help previewing or downloading a file from the website, scroll up to the text line (above the book cover image) that reads "Need help? Click here." and click on the highlighted text. When you are ready to proceed with your preview or download, hit the "Back" button on your browser menu to return to the *The Pastor's Guide to Weddings and Funerals* page.

This material is formatted using key words and extensive headings as listed in the table of contents. Need some guidance on ethical issues? See the section on ministerial ethics in the introduction. Need some direction on the format of a funeral service? See chapter 5 under Organizing the Funeral Service. Haven't performed a wedding for a while and need a refresher on the legalities, particularly of out-of-state (or province) weddings? See the section on legal requirements under weddings. Need resources gathered into one place so that you can easily pull together relevant Scriptures, a sermon outline, prayers, and benedictions? Download the information you need from the Judson Press website, add your own collection of resources, and then print out your own creation, fully fitted to your own situation.

This field manual does not pretend to be the final word on weddings and funerals. Ministry and its corresponding challenges are constantly and rapidly changing, making any "final" word obsolete by printing time. This resource does, however, form a solid base of "experience" for any pastor, a resource he or she will be able to build on over the years of ministry ahead.

May you, the reader, find this field manual an "experience" tool to mentor, enrich, and simplify your wedding and funeral preparation, as well as to inform your ethical decision-making.

Introduction

---~ᴓᴓ~---

The Challenging Context of Ministry

ON THE BROAD SPECTRUM, ministers are called by God to influence the spiritual awakening and formation of individuals, particularly members of the flock under their care. Bursting into this already extremely challenging context are two often unscheduled and, equally often, unreimbursed tasks. These two events are weddings and funerals, which tend to arrive on their own initiative. How challenging for the minister to transform what comes as an interruption into an opportunity for quality ministry. What creative time management it takes to plan a schedule flexible enough that these interruptions are nurtured into opportunities for spiritual growth. How accessible resources must be so valuable time is not wasted looking through files upon files, books upon books, for the right analogy, the right Scriptures, the right sermon thoughts. This manual is written to help facilitate these latter needs.

In seeking to move from "interruption" to significant ministry, many ministers admit to having a love/hate relationship with weddings and funerals. On the love side, these events are seen as two of the most sacred experiences a pastor will share with those under his or her care and ministry. Both instances present the opportunity for the masks of formality to be removed, allowing ministry to happen on an incredibly intense, deep level, a level that may otherwise take years to establish through normal church attendance and association. Thus the pastor is forced to admit that it is crucial to strive for one's most effective ministry during these sacred moments, thereby maximizing spiritual formation in the participants as well as bringing glory to God.

On the hate side, however, the pastor is forced to juggle labor-intensive ministry to the often small group involved while also maintaining ministry to the whole congregation. In other words, all regular pastoral duties are expected to continue despite the time-consuming intrusion. Having a "surprise" wedding appear on the schedule by a drop-in couple, or a funeral, which always occurs on its own time schedule, tends to put a pastor on overload. It is like having two Sundays in one week. An extra sermon needs to be prepared, worship elements need to be developed, and quality time needs to be spent with the families involved. The extra stress easily fuels one's hate side.

Significantly adding to the stress are the ethical considerations that tend to come with the leaving/cleaving partners or the grieving survivors. In other words, each event comes with its own agenda. The couple intending to wed may have no intention of following God. Yet, as a formality, they desire God's blessing on their marriage. The survivors of the deceased may not want God mentioned in the funeral, though it is to be held in a church and conducted by a minister. Thus an ethical dilemma is abruptly thrust into the pastor's lap. With time already tight, where can one turn for experienced, helpful advice toward making wise, ethical choices, toward even discerning that an ethical issue exists? "Discerning the dangerous obstacles lurking in this less-than-ideal world, like spotting fallen boulders on a mountain road, requires keen eyesight and constant vigilance."[1]

Allow this manual to suggest responses to these concerns and others, forming a beginning point for "constant vigilance." More in-depth guidance is offered through the resources listed in the annotated bibliography.

Ethical Guidelines

The young minister felt pressured by the family—prominent members of the church—to overlook the fact that their pregnant daughter was marrying a non-Christian. "You simply have to do the wedding and in our church," they insisted.

When it comes to ethical choices, where could this young minister turn for help and guidance? One place to start is with a review of one's own ministerial code of ethics. The second is to have a grid of practical, principle-based questions on which to reflect.

Ministerial Code of Ethics

Remember that denominational code of ministerial ethics you signed at ordination or upon induction as minister of your current church? (Joe Trull and James Carter have an excellent sampling of such codes, together with practical guidance on personalizing such a code, in the appendixes of their book *Ministerial Ethics: Being a Good Minister in a Not-So-Good World.*)[2] Refreshing yourself on these basic commitments is a good place to begin when considering ethical issues surrounding weddings and funerals. It is also helpful to approach this task with the attitude that being "a good minister has always meant more than just maintaining minimal standards."[3]

Another helpful resource is a personal philosophy of ministry statement. As you wrestled with developing this during your pastoral training, hopefully you began to flesh out your own convictions and applications on the ethical issues surrounding weddings and funerals. (Your personal stand on divorce and remarriage would be an example.) While this philosophical statement need not be your final word, it is a helpful place to begin clarifying real-life issues and your options.

Reviewing where you have stood in the past and where you are called to stand by your denomination or congregation, is a helpful place to begin your current quest for guidance on ethical issues surrounding weddings and funerals. The following questions may aid in furthering this quest.

Helpful Questions to Ask Regarding a Specific Ethical Issue

You have looked at your code of ethics and seminary papers but still feel stuck with regards to your current issue. Now what? Allow me to suggest four simple questions for self review that will help in the process of seeking appropriate ministry behavior and use of time when responding to wedding and funeral requests. These four questions, listed in order of importance, are:

- How can I be true to God and the Scriptures?
- How can I be true to myself and my calling?
- How can I be true to the church I am serving?
- How can I be true to the individuals involved?

Now let us consider each question in more detail.

How Can I Be True to God and the Scriptures?

As evangelicals, we use a variety of terms to describe how to be true to God in our actions, both personally and in ministry-related situations. For example, we speak in terms of "What is God's will in this situation?" "How would Jesus act in this situation?"

"Is following this particular course of action in keeping with God's character?" or "Can I honestly say I am doing all to the glory of God as I proceed?" Each of these important checks and balances can be helpful when trying to flesh out what would please God in the specific wedding or funeral situation you face.

The second aspect of this question, being true to the Scriptures, refers to following the whole of Scripture, not only isolated verses, in ministry. As you compare the message of the Bible as you understand it with your planned action, do the two coincide? Ask, "Is my interpretation accurate?" "Does God's Word speak to this particular issue?" (Scripture tends not to say, "Yes, Joe should marry Jane.") Certainly God's Word speaks most clearly concerning issues of integrity and honesty. How do those principles apply to weddings and funerals? Other issues, however, such as divorce and remarriage, are more difficult to understand, resulting in a variety of theological interpretations. (See chapter 1 under The Couple in Which One or Both Are Divorced.) It is helpful for ministers to work through these interpretations personally and to develop our own convictions before a situation arises in which we are pressured to make a choice. Once you have identified your own convictions, it is important to review them periodically and to respect your equally sincere colleagues when they arrive at a different understanding of these same passages. We must each live by the standard we have chosen.

How Can I Be True to Myself and My Calling?

This question has to do with the interaction of a pastor's own personal sense of well-being, personal convictions, and inner peace from the Holy Spirit. A sense of well-being is that "gut-level," intuitive sense you have about the rightness or wrongness of a situation. As ministers, we need to listen to our own heart as it directs us to draw back or extend grace.

Personal convictions are those applications of Scripture that we have personally wrestled through and chosen. They do not have the same authority as Scripture, since they are binding on us alone, but we still need to be true to them (or revise them) to maintain a clear conscience regarding our involvement, and resulting blessing, on the situation with which we are dealing. Two examples for some ministers would be, What if alcohol is to be served at the reception? and What if there is to be dancing at the reception and the couple wishes to use the church hall?

A sense of well-being, personal convictions, and, most important, an inner peace from the Holy Spirit, help you find the right response. What inner sense do you have from God about this specific course of action? Do you have any feeling of compromise, or do you feel like you are being used? If so, then you need further investigation and prayer concerning the issue before choosing a course of action.

While a pastor's calling is to minister to everyone for whom Christ died and to do so for God's glory, we also need to set boundaries and reserve the right to say no. In some situations it may well be more beneficial ministry to say no to a particular wedding than to go along with it and condone an unethical choice. Likewise, conveying false information at a funeral because the family desires to leave a better impression conflicts with the calling to proclaim truth.

How Can I Be True to the Church I Am Serving?

The church (or churches) each of us serves has its own culture and expectations. When you entered into covenant with your congregation, you agreed to work within that context. You should not take this commitment lightly when asked to lead a wedding or funeral that may offend this congregation or place this church in a bad light. We must also not be held hostage by unrealistic or unreasonable expectations. For example, suppose your honest searching has found a "green light" on the first two questions: How can I be true to God and the Scriptures? and How can I be true to myself and my calling? But now you are made clearly aware that proceeding would bring you into conflict with the church's view. What then? Common courtesy would say that the pastor should evaluate the merit and strength of the church's perspective. On what is the church's view based? Is it scriptural? Is there more history here than you know? And is this view really that of the majority or simply the opinion of an outspoken few? Another helpful area to focus on is: How will my ongoing ministry in this church be affected by my decision to proceed? Is proceeding worth it? Is this stand worth losing my position and ministry? What would be a healthy compromise?

Whenever pastors choose to proceed against the apparent wishes of our church, it is best to have at least the deacons or elders behind us. In other words, choose your battles wisely.

How Can I Be True to the Individuals Involved?

This guideline has to do with the desires, intentions, and spiritual commitment level of the individuals with whom you are working. For example, you would not be truthful if you preached an obviously unrepentant sinner to heaven in a funeral service, or if you indicated in your wedding commentary that a couple has a strong commitment to God, when it is well known they have no intention of pursuing their faith. It is also unethical to put words of deep spiritual commitment in people's mouths during their vows when they do not have a personal relationship with Christ nor any intention of serving him. Services must be adapted appropriately to the people involved, carefully working with their desires, intentions, and commitments. In some situations, a nonchurch service may be the most appropriate, such as a home wedding or a funeral chapel memorial service.

Ethical guidelines are an essential tool when seeking wisdom and guidance in ministry. Our ministerial code of ethics, our personal convictions, and these four helpful questions as listed are a useful grid in processing the ethical choices that come our way. Having outlined the grid, let us now consider its application.

Ethical Application

It is especially gratifying, when looking at a funeral or wedding service we have just finished preparing, if we can honestly feel that none of our ethical grid was compromised. Certainly this is a worthy ideal toward which we should strive. In real life, however, as often as not, honesty may well produce a mixed response. For example, "Yes, I am appeasing the individuals involved, as well as their relatives in the church, but I feel like I have sold out God and myself." Here we have an ethical problem, since an affirmative response to the first two questions, being true to God and myself, are more important than only a yes to being true to the individuals involved.

An equally disconcerting situation is when our colleagues may choose to resolve an ethical issue differently than us. For example, we are unsure as to where the deceased stood with regard to his or her personal salvation, so we voice that it is up to God whether this individual will be received into heaven. Our colleague chooses to encourage the family by giving the individual the benefit of the doubt and preaching God's grace. Are we able to hold our ethical views, allow others to hold theirs, and still respect one another in the wideness of God's kingdom?

Personal convictions and ethical norms will vary among individual pastors as we all seek to minister in God's name. Weddings and funerals will challenge these convictions and ethical norms on an uncomfortably regular basis.

Let us now consider, in two separate sections, some specific ethical situations that arise in weddings and funerals, seeking to apply these ethical principles to each opportunity for ministry.

Notes
1. *Joe E. Trull and James E. Carter,* Ministerial Ethics: Being a Good Minister in a Not-So-Good World *(Nashville: Broadman and Holman, 1993), 14.*
2. *Ibid., appendixes.*
3. *Ibid., 15.*

PART I

Weddings

{ 1 }

Wedding Ethics

———

BEING ASKED TO CONDUCT someone's wedding is a tremendous honor. Second only to our commitment to the Lord, the marriage covenant is intended to last a lifetime. What a privilege to lead someone in vows of such depth. Approaching the threshold of marriage, our own or that of a ceremony we are conducting, draws an appropriate sense of awe. Will this healthy sense of awe remain with us throughout the years of conducting wedding ceremonies?

I speculate that if ministers' feelings toward weddings were placed on a continuum, the two endpoints would look something like this. On one end is the opposite of awe, looking at the sacred task as "just another wedding." Unfortunately, some pastors' attitudes (or perhaps each of us at one low point or another) fall into this category. Whether from time pressures, overload, or general lack of interest ("I wish I didn't have to do weddings at all"), some pastors retaliate by "winging it" when it comes to weddings. They think, *Let's just get the old notes out and do a generic wedding.* Is that all God expects of us for such a sacred moment in a couple's life? Does this not become an ethical issue if we do not take the task seriously and make it special for the couple?

On the other end of the emotional continuum is an over-powering and immobilizing sense of awe. *I am helping this couple make a lifelong commitment. What happens if I mess up? What if they shouldn't be making this commitment at all, and I go ahead with the ceremony?* Panic can all too easily set in, sabotaging the pastor's diligent preparations and resulting in a very stilted, legalistic "read from the book so I can get it exactly right" type ceremony.

Of course, somewhere between these two extreme end-points of the continuum is the healthier place to be. Choose to feel the awe of the seriousness of marriage yet allow liberty of the Spirit to freely put yourself and everyone else at ease. Make the event both worshipful and a celebration—that is a good balance. Working through some of the ethical issues concerning marriage ahead of time will help bring you to this point of balance.

No doubt we all would agree that ministers are called to be ethical. And most of us sincerely desire to be ethical. The struggle comes when we try to define what is ethical in the current wedding situation before us. Thus it is helpful to think through areas of challenge before finding yourself in the midst of them so that when you do face them you have the necessary background to make solid decisions. Note that I did not say, "so that you will have all the answers." It is much easier to have a list of the types of weddings you will and will not do. Such a list may make your life easier, but by adhering to such a list, you will eliminate opportunities to minister to an increasing number of hurting people. A healthier approach is to study the issues, be aware of the ethical implications, and then make a seasoned decision on each specific case, given the factors involved in each particular situation.

Ethical Standards for Performing Ceremonies

Let's consider some typical marriage scenarios that ministers face and discuss the implications of applying the ethical grid of principles developed in the introduction.

Christian Marrying Christian

Are there any ethical issues surrounding the marriage of two Christians? In a perfect world, no. In our less-than-perfect world, maybe. For example, does each person have a genuine commitment to the Lord, or is one going along with "religion" to appease (and marry) the other? Since people tend to put their best foot forward, especially in striving for what they want, it may be difficult to tell when someone is faking Christianity. Spending a significant amount of time in premarital counseling with a couple helps clarify the depth of faith being proclaimed. Too often a "Christian couple" marries, and then six months later one drops out of church, soon followed by the other, because their true selves have emerged. How can you help keep members of your flock from "selling out" their faith in this way? The task is difficult, to be sure, but very much a part of your ethical responsibility to them as their pastor. Premarital counseling is a good setting in which to share with the couple any "red flags," you see. Even when their hearing is "dulled by love," you need to voice your concerns and let the Holy Spirit take it from there.

Another area to consider, given that both potential spouses are Christians, is how their spiritual maturity compares. Sometimes it works for the more mature Christian to disciple the newer one, and sometimes it does not. Though there is no biblical reason not to marry such a couple, you may well advise them to wait a while before marrying to give their faith a chance to grow and for them to become more in balance with each other. Then both of them will bring greater spiritual richness to the marriage.

Another issue to determine when marrying two Christians is whether they are in love or simply doing what is expected of them. Sometimes, in the church, we push two young people together because we think they are right for each other and would make a great team for God. We must allow couples to make this major commitment decision themselves and when they are ready rather than pushing them into it. How powerful it is for the pastor to intercept some of the pushing and buy the couple time to make up their own minds.

Another area that is increasingly becoming important among Christians preparing to marry is this: Does one have a call to ministry and, if so, how does the other feel about it? Will he or she share that call? In the past a call to ministry meant that both spouses saw that call as God's chosen vocation for them. In the traditional case both husband and wife had strong expectations placed on them, and both worked for the church, though only one was paid. In recent years we have seen a great shift from this pattern. Desiring to pursue their own careers, spouses who have spent time and energy developing their own skills are less willing to give these resources to the church for free. While dual career couples are becoming more acceptable in the church, they often are left with an extra challenge, for congregations still hold expectations regarding the nonministerial spouse's involvement in the church. How will the couple handle these expectations? Is only one called of God and not the other? Will they simply make it clear in their call to a church that only one is being hired? Will they negotiate the expectations so as to draw the support of the church? Will they ignore the expectations and hope they go away? (They won't.) Pastoral counsel is essential to helping a couple identify and resolve these issues.

Even when it comes to marrying a Christian to a Christian,

the pastor must answer the crucial ethical question, "Am I being true to God and the Scriptures by marrying this couple?" Two sub-questions to help answer this major one are "What is the potential of this particular marriage?" and "Am I working with or against God's will in blessing this union?"

Christian Marrying Non-Christian

If, during an interview, it becomes clear that one member of the couple is committed to the Lord and the other is not, should you proceed with wedding plans for them? The scriptural warning in 2 Corinthians 6:14 must be considered carefully: "Do not be bound together with unbelievers; for what partnership have righteousness and lawlessness, or what fellowship has light with darkness?"

Although this verse appears straightforward, applying it involves ethical choices. For example, some people would choose to balance it with verses such as 1 Corinthians 7:14: "For the unbelieving husband is sanctified through his wife, and the unbelieving wife is sanctified through her believing husband; for otherwise your children are unclean, but now they are holy."

Certainly this latter verse makes room for the Christian–non-Christian marriage, but the context appears to refer to an existing situation in which one partner has come to faith and the other has not followed. It would be stretching the meaning of the verse to use it as scriptural permission to enter a Christian–non-Christian marriage.

Another pastoral response to marrying a believer to an unbeliever is that some pastors feel that premarital counseling is an excellent opportunity to witness to the non-Christian. Although some pastors have led unbelievers to the Lord during premarital counseling, you have no guarantee that this will happen. Thus you are placed in a dilemma. Will you go ahead with the counseling until just before the wedding—letting the couple assume you will perform the ceremony—to see if the unbeliever makes a decision for Christ? Or will you speak clearly at the outset about the need for a commitment and risk having the unbeliever "fake" a decision so that you will go ahead with the wedding? Each couple is different and requires customized counsel. One thing I have found useful is to meet with the Christian individually and share with him or her my biblical concerns about the marriage. In one particular case, several other spiritual leaders in our church did the same thing, and the bride ended up calling off the wedding.

To perform a ceremony for a Christian and a non-Christian is a tough ethical decision, and it must be made by the pastor while trying to balance God's guidelines and grace. Again, it is helpful to wrestle with this issue before being in the middle of a situation in which you may be pressured to perform a ceremony for the deacon's daughter, of whom it is said, "But she is such a nice, clean-living girl." Here the ethical theme is being true to God and the Scriptures.

Non-Christian Marrying Non-Christian
The primary question in this ministry opportunity is, Why does the couple want a church wedding? Why do they want God's blessing on their union? Is it to appease a "religious" relative? Is it a family heritage moment? Is it because they like the architectural design of your church? Or is it the stirring of reawakening faith?

Spending time with the couple in premarital counseling will help ferret out the answer. In this case, perhaps it is best to side with grace. Since the wedding event is significant, sharing it with a couple may build a bond that could well become the couple's bridge to God.

Other ethical issues concern what Christian blessing is meaningful to those of limited or no commitment and what vows and prayers are appropriate (certainly not, "Lord, be the center of their home")? All three of the latter ethical questions are impacted by our choices: How can I be true to myself and my calling? How can I be true to the church I am serving? How can I be true to the individuals involved?

The Underage or Very Young Couple

Go to any public place (or any pediatrician's clinic), and you will see very young mothers and fathers—children raising children. Some of these young couples choose to marry. How are you to respond when the young, often immature, come to be wed?

Premarital counseling is particularly crucial for very young couples. Teenage marriages, especially when coupled with a child on the way or already born, face tremendous odds against creating a lasting marriage. The young couple needs all the support and guidance they will accept from a pastor. Work with them. Show them love. Help them through the premarital sessions to make good choices for their future concerning whether to marry or remain single and whether to give up the child for adoption. Guide them in making those choices and in taking responsibility for their choices rather than leaving them feeling forced by circumstances into a situation neither wanted.

Even when no child is involved, some couples still choose to marry right out of high school or during their senior year. This trend may even be culturally or regionally expected among some families. One of the greatest challenges such a couple will face is that each partner will change much over the next seven to ten years. With all the changes life experiences and maturing brings, the person they thought they knew is often replaced by a stranger. Many young marriage partners will desire to spread their wings and free themselves from family responsibility, to be the teenager they always wanted to be, placing a great strain on their marriage. Many are naively idealistic, thinking they will live on love and having no concept of how much it costs to play house for real.

For the rocky road ahead, help each couple see as much as they are open to see. Provide them with tools to mature together. Work with the families involved. As far as possible, help dissipate at least some of the blindness of young love. Especially seek to build strong bridges to them so that they can readily access help during the challenges ahead.

Most states and provinces require parental consent if either marriage partner is under eighteen years of age. This requirement will emerge when the couple goes to the courthouse to obtain their marriage license. Since picture identification is required, it is unlikely, though not impossible, for the couple to deceive their way past this civil law checkpoint. They also are required to sign an oath stating that all the information they have given to obtain the license is accurate.

North Dakota, for example, will not issue a marriage license to anyone under sixteen years of age. Those between sixteen and eighteen need both parents or a legal guardian to appear in person and sign a consent form before a marriage license will be issued. If either party is divorced, a certified copy of the finalized divorce is also required.

The Couple Already Intimate or Living Together

The most common ethical issue facing ministers today is the couple coming to be married who are already sexually intimate and who may be living together. How should a minister respond to this open and ongoing defiance of such Scriptures as: "Let marriage be held in honor among all, and let the marriage bed be undefiled; for fornicators and adulterers God will judge" (Hebrews 13:4) and "Now the deeds of the flesh are evident, which are: immorality, impurity, sensuality ... those who practice such things shall not inherit the kingdom of God" (Galatians 5:19,21)?

One response to this "common law" situation is to simply refuse to perform such weddings. This stance would maintain the law of Scripture but would also prohibit ministry to perhaps more than half the couples who come to us, never mind leaving theose individuals in their sin. This appears to be a lose-lose response.

Another response is to ask the couple to live separately and to abstain from sexual intimacy until the wedding, especially if the couple claims to be Christian and concerned about doing God's will. The dilemma for the minister is how far your responsibility extends. Is it sufficient to simply point out their sinful ways and allow them to respond in repentance to God as they are convicted of their sin? Or should a pastor's performing of the wedding be made conditional on the couple's obedience to God's Word? What if the couple simply refuses to separate? Or what if they say they will separate but do not? How could anyone even begin to monitor their separation or abstinence?

This issue begins as a "being true to God and the Scriptures" concern, but once the couple has been taught what God's Word says about having premarital sexual relations, it becomes a "remain true to myself and my calling" issue: *Will I, or will I not, perform the ceremony if the couple is still sexually intimate up to the wedding date?*

Certainly the couple's attitude about the matter must be taken into account. Open defiance of God's law devalues having a Christian ceremony. Perhaps a justice of the peace would be appropriate in such a case.

Another response, which may be more of a win-win resolution, is to work with the couple toward a more immediate, private wedding. A public ceremony could follow later. In certain cases, particularly when the couple already has had a child together, this response may well be most appropriate.

The Couple That Is Expecting a Baby

In bygone days this ethical situation was resolved with the bride's father or older brother showing up at the wedding with a shotgun. Although forcing a couple to marry in this way was extremely negative, one slim positive was that everyone was honest and open about what had happened.

Today a shotgun wedding is as inappropriate as ever, but sadly, honesty is also often considered old-fashioned. Honesty thus becomes an ethical issue that falls directly on the minister. An out-of-wedlock pregnancy makes the private sin of premarital sex public. Should it be more publicly acknowledged as well? If the couple has been sexually active, resulting in a pregnancy, should an apology be made at a specially called church meeting, as some congregations require? (I raise this issue to question it, not to reccommend it.) Or is a private confession before the elders sufficient? Or is simply telling the pastor of a private confession to God all that is needed?

Some sincere form of confession prior to the wedding date will bring a healthier beginning to the marriage. Scripture promises that God is faithful to forgive when we confess our sins (1 John 1:9), and such forgiveness bring healing—to the couple's relationship with God and in their own marriage relationship. This health will be beneficial to the couple as they cope with adjusting simultaneously to marriage and a baby and will also garner support from the church.

To a certain extent, this becomes a "true to the church I am serving" issue. What are the "rules" in your congregation? Are they appropriate and something you endorse as a minister? (If not, work on changing them before they are needed.) Rules help to insure that everyone is treated equally. They prevent the less fortunate from becoming a spectacle while the sin of those in prominent families is overlooked.

Keeping secrets is seldom healthy, especially a secret that will become evident a few months down the road. Others, however, feel that privacy is to be guarded and that couples have every right to choose their response to their predicament. But even so, once the couple has made their choice, the pastor must now also choose. You need to remain true to yourself and your calling. What does your value system call for in the public expression of honesty?

The Couple Whose In-laws Resist the Wedding

"He's just not good enough for my darling little baby!" "She's not perfect enough. My precious son deserves better!" "They have nothing in common. They will never become a couple. They are already fighting all the time."

The list of criticisms goes on and on. Was a bride or groom ever created perfect? Only in a parent's eyes. While we all know that no one is perfect, sometimes this standing is expected of the future son-in-law or daughter-in-law. How are pastors to discern between unrealistic expectations and legitimate concern as we work with struggling couples? How are we to respond when one set of parents threatens to leave the church if the ceremony takes place?

An important place to begin on this issue is to hear all sides of the story individually. Listen to the couple themselves, individually or together as appropriate, to hear their view of a parent's resistance to the wedding. Then privately interview each set of parents to hear their story. While listening, seek to have them stick to expressing their own views rather than projecting and interpreting the in-laws' views. With the information you gather you will be able to develop an initial sense of what is legitimate concern and what is unrealistic expectations. Discerning the honesty of all sides of the story is also crucial.

Based on the gathered information, the pastor may choose to meet a second time with each couple individually, to share "the rest of the story" and invite comment. This is especially helpful when misconceptions have arisen. Or the pastor may choose to meet solely with the couple planning to marry, lay out the various concerns causing the resistance, and help them work out the difficulties. This is helpful when a breakdown in communication has occurred and parents feel unheard. Still another alternative is to have the three couples meet together, with the pastor moderating the interaction, to work out concerns. This is especially important when each needs to hear the concerns and feelings of the others. Individual situations will influence which of these options, or an entirely different one, is the best choice.

Where the concerns expressed are legitimate, making them overt, rather than covert, is very healthy. Bringing harbored feelings and concerns to the foreground provides the couple with knowledge of what they are committing themselves to and gives them an opportunity to begin working on the problems. It also helps them make a better choice, especially if postponing the wedding may be in the best interest of all. You must be very careful, however, during this negotiation process, not to put control in the wrong person's hand, for example, the parent not ready to "let my baby go."

The Couple in Which One or Both Are Divorced

Two major issues arise when marrying divorced persons. The first, having to do with legal requirements, is more easily handled. Each U.S. state or Canadian province has rules regarding remarriage. In many provinces of Canada, a decree absolute must be produced by the divorced person to show that the divorce is final. Receiving this decree as part of the divorce settlement usually involves a two-year waiting process from the time the divorce was filed. Fortunately for the minister, this document is required to obtain a new marriage license, so the minister may not have to deal with it at all, unless a couple is dishonest when obtaining the license. Though currently considering similar waiting periods, many states now simply require that the divorce process be finalized. Since divorce laws regularly change, you will want to check with the local courthouse for laws concerning divorce and remarriage in your area.

The second issue has more to do with ministerial ethics. The Bible says that God hates divorce (Malachi 2:16) and that divorce is permissible only where unfaithfulness has occurred (Matthew 19:3–9). But does unfaithfulness refer only to sexual unfaithfulness, or does it include faithless behavior such as physical abuse, mental abuse, desertion, and so on? And even when divorce is permissible, is the person free to remarry? Those who work from a model of God's grace will say yes. Those who work from a model of God's law will say no. Pastors would be wise to work through these issues before being confronted with a divorce and remarriage situation so that we can make sound decisions when needed. Like personal convictions, chosen ministerial ethics are extremely helpful guidelines (not laws) to aid you in making God-honoring choices when ministering to a sinful world. Seek to balance God's law and God's grace in each individual situation.

The Couple in Which One or Both Already Have Children

While this scenario does not normally raise ethical concerns for ministers, life's quirks can raise concerns here. For example, suppose a younger person plans to marry an elderly, wealthy individual and the grown children of that older individual come to us as their pastor to ask for help in fighting the union. Here the concern is "How can I be true to the individuals involved?" You may share the children's suspicions concerning the relationship and choose not to perform the ceremony (although this may not stop the wedding). Or you may side with the couple (when they really do love each other and could enjoy significant years of happiness, and the children are the greedy ones). A prenuptial agreement may also be appropriate when arranged fairly and freely. While some individuals may feel such an agreement compromises "becoming one," others see it simply as rewriting the will, taking into account the new relationship.

A more common situation is when teenage or younger children adamantly oppose a parent's remarriage, hoping that Mom and Dad will get back together. In such a scenario, you may want to suggest slowing down the time schedule and, through counseling, help the potential stepfamily work through their fear, anger, guilt, unrealistic expectations, and so on. The goal would be to have the wedding become a joyful climax to the work everyone has done. Involving the children in a meaningful way in the vows or in the giving of the bride is very appropriate. Making everyone happy, however, may simply not be possible. Pastoral care will need to be appropriate and ongoing.

The Interracial Couple

Different cultures advocate different practices, and these can cause conflicts within marriages. For example, one woman's culture called for a child-rearing practice involving "walking out one's fear." Even toddlers were placed in scary situations so that they learned to curb and control their fear. To illustrate, a child afraid of heights was made to totter along the edge of a cliff until the fear vanished. This practice was considered good parenting in the woman's culture, but her potential American spouse did not agree. Without premarital counseling, such issues as parenting styles would probably not come up for discussion prior to the wedding.

Race is not to be a barrier to marriage. Certainly the equality of all people before God is a biblical concept. When it comes to interracial marriages, then, your ethical responsibility is more in the area of pointing out practical issues to the couple. For example, how well does the couple understand each other's culture with regards to family life? If one culture is matriarchal and the other patriarchal, leadership in this marriage will need to be negotiated.

What are the values, norms, and mores surrounding expectations of husband and wife? In some cultures it is acceptable to have more than one wife. In others the practice of having a mistress is not only accepted but encouraged. What will the couple agree on as right and wrong for their marriage?

What are the husband's and wife's role expectations as taught by the individual's culture? Which will be applied in this marriage, either intentionally or unconsciously? In some cultures the woman may participate actively in the business world, climb the corporate ladder, and be coequal with her spouse. In another culture the wife remains at home, goes out in public only with a veiled face, and needs an escort. In still other cultures, the wife's role is to serve the husband and be completely self-sacrificing. Resolving a couple's cultural differences may require much discussion and negotiation.

"But we live in America. We will do as the Americans do." Nice thought but naively idealistic. Though the couple may now live in America, cultural baggage tends to come along. Will the couple adapt to a harmonious cultural compromise, or are they headed for an explosion? Allowing the couple to enter marriage blind to their cultural differences and biases would be unethical for a minister.

On the other hand, helping the couple work through cultural issues before the wedding will strengthen the marriage. It will also enable them to incorporate meaningful cultural elements into the wedding ceremony itself. Guide them in customizing their wedding, but remember that there is little value in enacting a traditional, cultural ceremony only for appearances. Sensitivity to the couple's cultures, choices, and parents, however, is important. Thus a delicate balance needs to be found.

The Interfaith Couple

An interracial marriage is more complicated when two different faiths are involved. (Note that I am not referring to different Christian denominations.) An interfaith marriage becomes an ethical issue for the minister when two world religions are involved, such as Christianity and Buddhism, for example. Are there many paths to God as long as a person is sincere? Our pluralistic society encourages this idea, and even individual Christians have differing theologies on this point. An evangelical minister who affirms that Christ is the only way to God (see John 14:6) must draw a line. In my view, the issue is one of "being true to God and the Scriptures."

Depending on your own beliefs and the convictions of the church you serve, this issue may well come back to the question, "Am I performing the ceremony for a Christian and a non-Christian?" (See above.)

Marriage of Convenience

Many people come from other countries with a desire to live in the United States. One way to "earn" the right to live here is to utilize the illegal practice of "arranging" a marriage of convenience. This involves finding a willing marriage partner to legally marry, continuing the relationship for two years, and then agreeing to divorce and go separate ways, citizenship having been attained. While the government continues to crack down on such unlawful practices, ministers may face them as well. Being somewhat suspicious at times will aid you in being "true to yourself and your calling" and will help you avoid being used by those wishing to skirt the law.

More difficult yet is when a church-sponsored refugee family, in trying to bring additional family members to the U.S. or Canada, is arranging such a marriage. Perhaps safety and survival of the relatives is at stake. Here "being true to myself and my call" may collide with "being true to the church I am serving" and "being true to the individuals involved." Personal integrity and sanctity of God-ordained marriage are at issue here as you try to remain ethical. What does being "faithful to God" mean for you in the situation at hand?

The Couple Using a Translator

While normally no ethical issues are involved in the case of a wedding couple using a translator because of a language barrier, the ethical challenge for the minister is to help everyone fully understand the vows of commitment being made, especially the bride and groom. This type of situation may also fall into the "marriage of convenience" category (see above) if the person not understanding English also does not fully understand the commitment being made. Thus an interpreter who can be trusted to make clear all that occurs in the sacred service is essential.

Communion in the Wedding Ceremony

Including Communion in the wedding ceremony was popular during the 1980s and '90s but has waned in recent years. The ethical dilemma for the pastor surrounds the worthiness of the couple in approaching God's table. Communion participants must come as repentant believers in Christ. If one or both of the partners are not believers yet desire to have Communion served in their wedding ceremony, the pastor must decide whether he or she is going to be "true to God and the Scriptures." The New Testament clearly warns against unworthy participation at the Lord's table: "Whoever eats the bread or drinks the cup of the Lord in an unworthy manner, shall be guilty of the body and the blood of the Lord" (1 Corinthians 11:27). Scripture holds no provision for relaxing the rules when it comes to wedding Communion.

Another complication in this scenario is when couples have a substantially different view of Communion. For example, if one is Protestant and the other Catholic, they need to discuss what Communion will mean for them in their wedding. A further ethical choice here for the pastor is, "If their view of Communion is different than mine, will I be true to myself and my calling if I conduct it?" Some would not see this issue as an ethical concern but would allow each to come to the Lord's table with his or her own beliefs. Personal convictions tend to guide this decision.

When the Minister Feels "Talked into" Performing a Wedding

"How can I be true to myself and my calling?" is seriously challenged in marriage situations that are not ethically black and white. If you are unable to put your finger on why you are reserved about performing a particular wedding, you should trust your instinct and do a little more digging. Usually this feeling arises around the "instant wedding," in which a couple relatively unknown to the pastor appears at the church door and desires to be married "right away." Having a strong conviction, and church policy, about walking them through premarital counseling first, is very helpful in dealing with this kind of questionable situation. Though the couple may simply find someone else to perform a ceremony on short notice, that is their choice. There are times when we need to extend grace, and there are other times when we need to listen to the still, small voice within and preserve our integrity and convictions.

Returning to a Former Church to Do a Wedding

Being asked to return to a former pastorate to perform a wedding is very appealing to the ego, but it is very unethical to do so without first contacting your successor in that church. He or she is their pastor now and hopefully will have an ongoing pastoral relationship with them. A wedding is a significant time for them to cement that pastoral relationship. The choices here are: (1) say no to the couple; (2) contact the current minister and share the service with him or her; or (3) contact the current minister and proceed only with his or her blessing. The second alternative is healthiest.

Pastoral Policy on Premarital Counseling

We live in a society in which people expect instant service, and unfortunately, this sometimes includes weddings. At some point in every pastor's career, we probably will receive a call asking if we can do a wedding "this afternoon" or "as soon as possible." Most likely there will be little or no association between the church and the couple, but bride and groom desire to be married in a church rather than by a justice of the peace.

Many pastors simply say no to such opportunities, and the brevity of such marriages tends to reinforce this decision. Yet the fact that a church wedding is even sought may well provide an entrance for ministry that otherwise would be unavailable. At least meeting with the couple for an initial interview to discuss the potential for counseling may be helpful.

Having a set church policy concerning premarital counseling

is useful in dealing with "hurry-up" marriages. My personal policy is to require at least six one-hour counseling sessions before performing a ceremony. In some churches my policy was backed by the church's governing board, which then made it a church policy. This strengthened my position and helped me be true to myself and my convictions. When couples were willing to come for counseling, a much more significant relationship developed between them and myself, opening more opportunities for ministry. When couples refused, I was spared compromising my conviction that premarital counseling is essential.

On the few occasions where I did compromise my policy, I either did postwedding counseling with the couple or reaffirmed in myself that next time I would stick to my policy. Hindsight showed that compromise was not justified. If ministers would stick together in requiring premarital counseling, couples would be prohibited from simply going down a list of pastors until they found one who would do a ceremony no questions asked.

One rationale for defending the need for premarital counseling is this: When we start any new job, we go through orientation to get acquainted with the job and our new environment. If we are willing to put time into preparation for what might be only a temporary job, how can we refuse six hours of orientation to a new lifestyle that is to last forever? I ask couples, "How serious are you about making this marriage work if you don't want to invest any time in orientation for it?"

From a very practical standpoint, premarital counseling sessions also provide a forum for leading the couple through the paperwork and planning associated with the wedding. Appendixes A, B, and C in this manual provide some basic forms that I use at my first meeting with a couple. The forms can be photocopied as they are or downloaded from the Judson Press website and modified for your own use.

Appendix A: Wedding Interview Guide

Refer to this form when a couple meets with you for the first time regarding getting married. Adapt the form to fit your needs as their potential minister, and use it as your guide for the interview rather than having them fill it out.

Appendix B: Procedural Guidance and Information Sheet

Most churches already have policy that governs weddings held in their facilities. This sheet may be used as a comparison against an existing policy or as a model to draft such a policy for your church. This informational sheet is a helpful way to suggest the going rates of remuneration for services rendered, whether for use of the church building or for the services of the organist, pastor, or other staff members.

Appendix C: Church Wedding Application Form

Use this form to confirm with the couple the booking of the church and use of additional services. Especially for Canadian weddings, this form also provides the information needed by the pastor to complete the government paperwork required of the minister.

The wedding scenarios presented in this chapter are the most common ones to challenge a minister's ethics. Most likely more unique ones will arise in your career. May you respond to each one effectively using your ethical grid to aid you in making wise choices.

{2}

Planning the Wedding

BECAUSE DIFFERENT PERSONALITIES are at work in each couple, each wedding is uniquely planned. Some people like to plan everything well in advance, including booking the church and the minister. Other couples tend to make all the plans and then ask the minister last, assuming that he or she and the church come as a package and are always available. Some couples have been church members since childhood; others pick the building for its stained glass, long aisle, or intimate seating. Some couples have elaborate plans for an intensely worshipful wedding ceremony. Still others have no concept at all of the potential impact of, or what is involved in, a church wedding.

Thus, as pastor, you may be called upon either to help with a wedding, starting from square one and explaining the basics, or to come alongside a fully and appropriately planned wedding service and simply fulfill your part. This manual provides suggestions for all levels of pastoral involvement, including various elements of the wedding ceremony, ideas for a variety of wedding settings, helpful hints for leading the wedding rehearsal, guidance for last-minute adjustments, and coping with (and avoiding) wedding bloopers.

Elements of the Wedding Ceremony

While individual elements in weddings may vary, common themes should form the basis of all weddings. Two themes around which a wedding should be planned are worship and the couple's unique tastes and culture.

A Service of Worship

First and foremost, the minister is called to make it clear that a marriage ceremony is a sacred service of worship. By choosing to use a representative of God, and perhaps God's house, the couple has invited God's presence at their wedding. They are purposely asking for God's blessing on the marriage. To stand in God's holy presence and invite God's participation involves worship.

Keeping worship as the central theme in the wedding ceremony is a great benefit in planning what is appropriate and what is not. For example, if worship of God is the theme, a secular rock music selection is inappropriate for the processional. Using the theme, rather than taste in music, as the guideline for accepting or rejecting ideas will help the pastor negotiate such items with the couple.

A Service Descriptive of the Couple

Another challenging aspect of negotiating the details of a wedding ceremony with the couple is to make the service descriptive of both the bride and groom. Often the groom likes to take the backseat and let the bride plan the ceremony. I encourage the groom to be involved in planning since this is his wedding too. What is representative of each person's tastes and culture? How could the ceremony be tailor-made rather than being a one-size-fits-all generic ceremony? The key is to match the service to the couple, authentically revealing their tastes, values, and spiritual commitment.

As for tastes, allow a couple's preference for country-style clothing rather than insisting on stiff, formal tuxedos. There is room for flexibility in most areas of taste. If, however, the groom wishes to sing a love song as part of the ceremony but has no singing ability, an alternative should be encouraged. Use discretion in developing the service with the couple.

Regarding values, if family is important to the couple, parents and siblings could be meaningfully involved. This may vary from reading Scriptures, to participating in the wedding party, to having a moment of silence in honor of a deceased parent. Further ideas are developed in chapter 3 of this manual.

Authentically portraying spiritual commitment involves honesty. For example, suppose one or both persons are just beginning to seek God. Making it sound like they are both deeply committed to God with a proven track record of spiritual maturity just to appease other family members is inappropriate. Instead, honestly draw out their current heart commitment and encourage growth from there. Avoid scolding them for where they "should be" spiritually.

If personalized vows are desired but the pastor knows neither couple will remember them at the crucial moment (few will, unaided), secure a copy of their vows ahead of time and be prepared to coach them as needed. Some wedding partners will only need a hint to start and/or continue. Some may need the minister to revert to traditional style and say each phrase, with the individual repeating after him or her. Knowing this level of help is available may reduce nervousness enough for the couple that the vows will flow smoothly as intended. Work with the couple to ensure the successful completion of their special service.

Main Ingredients and Optional Styles

I have found it helpful to have checklists of regular and optional wedding elements available. During premarital counseling, I

devote an entire session to planning the wedding. I walk
through the checklist with the couple, having them choose the
elements they desire in their ceremony and adding anything else
they would like. (See Appendixes D and E for the checklist
forms I created, which you may photocopy for your own use or
download from the Judson Press website.) Note that Canadian
services have some elements as a regular feature that U.S. services do not have.

Order of Worship

The Wedding Order of Worship Planning
Sheet (see Appendix D) features a list of the
traditional elements usually included in a
wedding ceremony—everything from the
musical prelude and seating of the mothers, to
the vows and exchange of rings, to the recessional and receiving line. Guide the couple through the list,
explaining any element with which they are unfamiliar and
helping them to identify which elements they want to include in
their own ceremony. The Order of Worship checklist also
includes a section for adding unique or special elements to the
service. Additions to the traditional ceremony, such as
Communion, tributes to the mothers of the couple, special
music, and so on, are discussed here.

Selected Order

While the elements on the planning form are listed in the order
in which they typically occur, the order may be varied to cus-
tomize the service. In the selected order, note that no longer is
there a place for "If anyone has any grounds for keeping this
wedding from proceeding, let them speak now or forever hold
their peace." This line was dropped some time ago from most
ceremonies, although some ministers still erroneously believe it

to be a legal or ethical requirement. Since wedding dates are usually published well in advance by formal wedding invitations and other public notices, people have ample time to raise any issues or legal concerns before the actual marriage. By ceremony time it is too late. Nevertheless, be prepared to address such an interruption in the service should it arise.

Other Details Concerning the Service

You will find the Wedding Service Format Checklist in Appendix E helpful for negotiating other wedding details. This checklist will encourage the bride and groom to consider their options and make decisions early about a multitude of options, some of which are discussed briefly below.

The bridal party and ceremony participants. The couple will need to consider carefully the persons whom they will invite to be members of the bridal party. Who will be the honor attendants (i.e., maid/matron of honor and best man)? How many other attendants (i.e., bridesmaids and groomsmen) will be involved? Do they want to ensure even numbers so every party member has an escort? Will they involve any children as junior attendants, flower girl(s), or ring bearer(s)? Be sure to verify the correct spelling of participants' names, so that legal forms can be completed properly and so the wedding bulletin, if being done by the church, can be prepared accurately. Asking the couple about who will play the organ or piano for the ceremony should communicate to them that such a service is not included in the church wedding package and thus that they will need to budget for the additional fee charged by a professional musician. The checklist also covers such details as the entrance of the bridal party (e.g., Who, if anyone, will escort the bride? Will the bridesmaids be accompanied down the aisle by the groomsmen?

Will the party process at a regular pace or in the more stately "hesitation step"?); the timing and location of such traditions as lighting the unity candle, partaking in communion, and signing the marriage register (Canadian service only). Too, the couple will need to make decisions about what vows they will speak (e.g., traditional, contemporary, original), what their married name(s) will be and how they want to be introduced to the congregation, whether they will allow flash pictures during the ceremony, whether they will prepare a formal wedding program/bulletin for their guests—and who will prepare this. Note that this structure is primarily for a church wedding. Details will need to be adjusted for different settings. (See Wedding Settings below for these suggestions.)

Signing of the register (Canadian services only). In Canada, part of the wedding legalities and ceremony involves the signing of the register. Discuss with the couple where and when this will take place on the day of the wedding. Some couples prefer that the signing be a public part of the ceremony itself. A special table may be set on the platform and covered with a special tablecloth—from one of the couple's grandmothers, perhaps. Alternatively, the couple and their legal-aged witnesses might withdraw with the pastor into the side office to sign the legal documents. If no office is immediately convenient to the sanctuary, another room may be used (e.g., choir or Sunday school room). Special music usually plays during this interval.

Allowance of flash pictures during the ceremony. Because a wedding is a service of worship, a multitude of flash pictures can be distracting, especially if guests come to the front of the sanctuary at the most intimate parts of the service. With the couple's approval, some caution should be verbally made at the beginning of the service, such as, "Please refrain from taking flash pictures from after the processional until the recessional." Guests may be invited to return to the sanctuary after the recessional and receiving line (if applicable) to take posed photographs of the couple reenacting significant parts of the service.

Vows. While many couples still choose to repeat the traditional vows, a variety of other options are now available. (See chapter 3 and appendix G for examples.) Some are more "modern" renderings of the traditional words (e.g., "you" for "thee," etc.). Others are contemporary promises or covenants that reflect new metaphors for married life and relationships in today's world. Provide the couple with some examples of contemporary vows. Entire books have been published that are compilations of these vows. Alternatively, some couples choose to write their own vows, or to modify the traditional or contemporary versions. It may be appropriate to offer some guidance to the couple as they put their vows into writing. Do insist upon securing a written copy of each partner's vows in case either party has a memory lapse and needs to be coached during the ceremony. Too, depending upon your ethical grid, denominational guidelines, and the couple's choice, the vows may become an ethical issue if the proposed commitments are not binding—such as, "until love do us part."

Publication of service order. Does the couple want a formal bulletin, listing all elements of the service and members of the bridal party and immediate family? If so, who will prepare this program? Be sure to discuss this so that the couple does not assume that the church will do this, while you are assuming that the couple is handling it! The other option is to have an informal order of worship held only by the pastor and pianist or organist.

Times. Do not neglect to discuss and establish firm dates and times for the wedding ceremony itself and the rehearsal. (You might use the application found in Appendix C as confirmation of this information; see also Appendix D.) Also consider when the bridal party and family may have access to the facility to decorate for the ceremony. When will the florist be delivering the flowers and who will be there to receive them? Too, if the reception will be held at the same location as the ceremony, talk with the couple about what time the food should be served, when that space will be available for setup, decoration, and food preparation.

Married name desired. How does the couple wish to be introduced to the congregation at the conclusion of the ceremony? Today's couple has a multitude of options available to them. Encourage them to consider the question early and make a decision as soon as possible. Will they follow tradition and have the bride take the groom's family name? If so, do they want to be introduced as "Mr. and Mrs. Harry Smith" or as "Mr. and Mrs. Harry and Jane Smith"? Will one or both of them hyphenate their last names, or will they each retain their own names? Do they want to be introduced as "Mr. and Mrs." or "Mr. and Ms."? Or would they prefer to be introduced without titles, as "Harry and Jane Jones-Smith"? Whatever an individual couple's choice, try to use their legal married name in your congregational introduction, and make sure you learn the correct pronunciation!

Using a checklist such as the one found in Appendix D can be very practical for any minister in helping a couple plan their wedding ceremony. Various options for each of these service ingredients are presented in chapter 3.

The Value of a Wedding Coordinator

No matter how well a wedding is planned, there comes that moment in the wedding service when you have taken your place at the front of the sanctuary and are helpless to pace the processional at the rear of the sanctuary. Thus a wedding coordinator is essential for coaching nervous flower girls and ring bearers, as well as for starting bridesmaids down the aisle at the appropriate times. This valuable person also looks after myriad other details the pastor should not need to be responsible for, such as opening the church for delivery of flowers and furnishings (candelabras, kneeling bench, arch, etc.), ensuring that dripless candles are used, and overseeing decorating of the sanctuary so that pews and other church furnishings are not damaged by adhesives, tacks, or other fasteners.

A good wedding coordinator can greatly ease the minister's stress and help ensure a truly worshipful ceremony. The coordinator may be someone associated with the church whose fee is included in the church package, someone hired independently by the bride and groom, or simply a volunteer—perhaps a family member or friend of the couple who is good with details. Be sure to involve the coordinator at the rehearsal as well. Such a person is especially a godsend when doing a wedding in a church with which you are unfamiliar.

Wedding Settings

The young couple beamed at the minister as they enthused, "We want to be married on the city bus!" As the pastor sputtered, the lovebirds described how they had met as regular passengers on a particular bus, and they had made arrangements to rent it for the wedding.

Good shock absorbers and flexibility are essential to ministry. Thankfully, although unique weddings make the news, few marriages actually begin this way. For those that do, the minister is called upon to balance personal flexibility with faithfulness to the sacredness of marriage. This manual will consider four common wedding settings: the church wedding, the outdoor wedding, the home wedding, and the private wedding.

Church Wedding

The most popular wedding setting, of course, is the church. Two questions a pastor needs to address are: "What is worshipful in this sanctuary?" and "How can this specific wedding (size, style, etc.) be best fit into this sanctuary space (logistically and aesthetically)?"

The first issue, what is worshipful in this sanctuary, primarily involves appropriateness and some experienced common sense. Appropriateness has to do with what is fitting in the presence of a holy God, albeit one who also has a sense of humor. As God's spokesperson, the pastor needs to help guide the couple to a healthy balance. Appropriateness also relates to the particular culture of the church being used. It would not be wise for you to ruffle a lot of feathers in the flock with whom you will remain long after the couple, and their imaginative ideas, have moved on.

Experienced common sense emerges from "having been there before." You learn many practical things about doing weddings

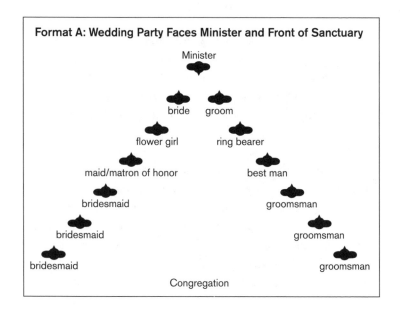

in a particular sanctuary; for example, that candles placed in a certain spot tend to blow out during the service due to drafts, or that the board of deacons is particularly sensitive to wax drippings on the carpet (use dripless candles) or thumbtacks in the pews (tie decorations on with wire or ribbon, or use tape or pliable adhesive that won't leave a residue). Good stewardship of the facility is part of your responsibility as pastor.

The second issue, regarding fitting a wedding party into the front of a particular sanctuary, can be a challenge, especially when a large wedding party is to be placed on a small, narrow platform. There are a variety of options (see diagrams below). A rehearsal prior to the wedding will be a tremendous help. Also very useful, even before the rehearsal, is to physically walk around on the platform with the couple to plan where everyone will stand. Doing this planning first gives the couple's views priority over all the other opinions that will be shared at the rehearsal.

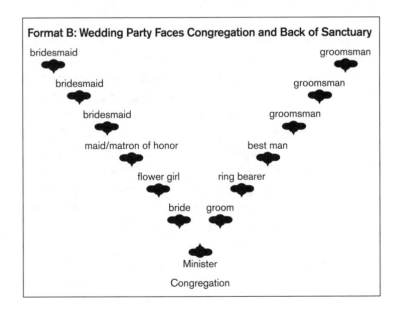

Format B: Wedding Party Faces Congregation and Back of Sanctuary

bridesmaid   groomsman

bridesmaid   groomsman

bridesmaid   groomsman

maid/matron of honor   best man

flower girl   ring bearer

bride   groom

Minister

Congregation

Depending on the particular sanctuary, the wedding party may face the minister and the front of the room, with the congregations at their backs. In this arrangement, the party might stand in a triangle such as illustrated in Format A, in a semi-circle, or on different levels if stairs limit platform space. Depending on their age and activity level, the flower girl and ring bearer could also be placed next to the person they know best in the wedding party so everyone can be more at ease.

The advantage of the rear-facing arrangement (illustrated in Format B) is that the congregation can see the bride and groom's faces throughout the service. The challenge is for the minister to be heard, since his or her back is to the congregation the entire time. Also, some ministers are uncomfortable with having the audience at their back.

Still other formats are feasible, such as the entire wedding party standing in a circle or the attendants standing together as couples. Creativity is valuable here, as choices and sanctuary space are adjusted to each other.

Outdoor Wedding

Often a couple chooses to challenge the weather and have their ceremony outdoors. When Mother Nature cooperates, the outcome is an absolutely beautiful wedding. Special considerations need to be made, however. For example, an effective sound system needs to be set up and pretested. Possible sound competition should be taken into account, such as highway noise, animal noise (if on a farm), and other possible distractions (such as neighbors in their swimming pool). Seating should be arranged so that all can see and hear. Also helpful, in very hot weather, is seating in the shade for those who cannot handle direct sunlight.

Moreover, a "plan B," an alternative place to hold the wedding, is necessary in case of inclement weather. This plan should be announced ahead of time, even in the invitations if possible, so that people are not lost in the transition.

Home Wedding

When a small wedding is the couple's choice, a home setting may be especially appropriate. This wedding can be very beautiful, though simple. Although there is seldom a formal rehearsal for a home wedding, it is helpful to explain to the participants the format that will be followed. Verbally walk through the sequence of events just prior to the ceremony so that participants have opportunity to ask questions. Careful explanations will set them at ease and prevent embarrassing mistakes, making the experience more meaningful and sacred.

Private Wedding (Couple and Witnesses Only)

Though traditionally the domain of the justice of the peace, sometimes couples choose a minister of the gospel to perform their private ceremony. Such simple spiritual openness deserves ministry.

The private wedding may be held in a church chapel, in a home (perhaps the minister's), or in the pastor's study. Again, care should be given to explain all that will occur so that the wedding will remain sacred and meaningful.

As with any wedding, you should ensure that the marriage documents (license and certificate) are present and in order. Two witnesses over the age of eighteen are required by law to sign these legal papers.

The Wedding Rehearsal

"Is another evening out really necessary? I've already put in all this extra work for this wedding; do I need to hold a rehearsal too?" Such questions often are raised when discussing the necessity of a wedding rehearsal.

The Need

No minister appreciates an unnecessary extra evening out away from his or her family. Wedding rehearsals are, however, very necessary. One of the greatest difficulties in conducting a wedding is dealing with everyone's nervousness, including the pastor's own. Just like a dress rehearsal for a stage drama, a wedding rehearsal clears away confusion, helps participants experience their parts, and provides an opportunity to tie up loose ends. For these reasons, a rehearsal is invaluable and greatly enhances the sacredness and pageantry of the wedding itself.

Who Is in Charge?

One of the interesting things about a wedding rehearsal is that a well-meaning, natural leader tends to emerge, fully enjoying directing everyone and instituting his or her idea of how the wedding should happen. Often one of the mothers will assume this role. But since this is not the mother's wedding, I recommend that the pastor take charge, before the natural leader is on a roll, to ensure that the couple's desires are carried out as planned. Other ideas should be appreciated and acknowledged but only used if appropriate. Careful leadership is needed here by the pastor so the rehearsal does not turn into a nightmare.

A Suggested Format

Ministers tend to develop their own style of conducting rehearsals. The method I have found most useful is threefold. Part one involves gathering everyone together, asking them to be seated, leading in an opening prayer, and then explaining the ceremony procedure. Walking through the events verbally first helps give everyone the big picture of how their part fits into the whole. It also provides an opportunity to explain the significance and sacredness of a wedding, deserving the best from each and every participant.

Part two involves actually doing the processional and other movements that will be part of the wedding. Stop as many times as necessary to make corrections (e.g., "You walked too fast; try again"), until all feel comfortable with their parts. Also use this time to introduce the significant musical pieces the wedding party will need to recognize. For example, "When you hear this song, the men and the pastor will enter." "When you hear this selection, the bridesmaids will enter." "When you hear this piece, the bride will proceed down the aisle." Helping participants to learn their cues will make the wedding go more smoothly. And having a coach at the back of the sanctuary during both the rehearsal and the wedding to help nervous wedding participants remember their cues also is of tremendous benefit. The wedding coordinator would be a good choice for this role.

Once everyone knows what he or she is doing, it is time for the third element, a "dress rehearsal." This time proceed through the entire wedding format without interruption as if it were the real thing. Tell people that if they make a mistake, they need to just keep on going like they will at the real wedding. Mistakes that come out here are less likely to come out in the wedding itself.

How much of the wedding should be practiced? On the third time, I like to include most elements, including special music, so that people have a feel for the whole service. Two things I do reserve, however, for the wedding itself, are the actual vows (in the rehearsal I simply explain the procedure we will follow, such as repeat after me) and my mini-sermon.

Many couples have a wedding party supper prior to the wedding. This works well in coordination with the rehearsal.

Coaching Wedding Ushers

One of the things we often take for granted in the church is the ability to usher. We assume that people just know how to usher well, and many do. If most, or all, of the ushers are from out of town, however, some orientation is practical. Explain to them where light switches are, where bathrooms are located in case someone asks them, how to seat people (offer your right arm to the women), and where to seat them (bride's family and friends on the left; groom's family and friends on the right). Invite them to be at the wedding at least a half hour early to begin their job. Encourage them to do their best and make people feel comfortable.

A good time for this brief orientation is during the rehearsal. Providing ushers with a handout listing times and duties is also very practical. (See Appendix F for an example.)

The "Moment" Is Almost Here

Ten minutes before the wedding, everyone is scurrying around, tittering nervously. The pastor still has two important jobs to do.

Calming and Supporting the Nervous

Your first job is to calm and support the nervous couple and the wedding participants in the final moments before the wedding. Mingle with the wedding participants. A word here, an appropriate touch there, a brief prayer if appropriate, but most of all a calm, comforting presence will greatly help the final preparations for the "big event." Of course, you too must be thoroughly prepared, ready to proceed, and personally at ease.

Last-Minute Details

Your second job is to check on last-minute details. Has every-one in the wedding party arrived? Remember, the musician will begin the cue music right on the designated hour unless some-one tells him or her there is a delay. The minister needs to be this connecting link, ensuring that everyone is ready to proceed. Make "the rounds" one final time. Tell everyone the wedding is about to start. As they move to their places, you must be ready to station yourself, signal the musician, and enter on cue. But remember to take the groom into the sanctuary with you. It is amazing how even the toughest guys develop jelly legs at this point and need the pastor's support, verbally and some-times even physically. Give him a shoulder to lean on to bolster his courage. Then lead the way forward into the sanctuary.

Coping with (and Avoiding) Wedding Bloopers

Even the best laid plans are sometimes interrupted by the ridicu-lous. Here are a few possibilities to anticipate arising in a wed-ding, with a plan B in case they do.

When Someone in the Wedding Party Does Not Show Up

The groomsman had arrived in town on time. He had picked up his tuxedo, and it fit. He had even attended the rehearsal and participated as expected. But, come the time of the wedding itself, he was no where to be found. Word came that he was not coming. The wedding was to start in fifteen minutes. The quick-thinking groom approached one of the ushers, also dressed in a tuxedo, though slightly different, and invited him to stand in for the delinquent groomsman. The usher was honored to accept and saved the day.

The lesson from this true story is that last-minute alternatives, though not perfect, can be found for wedding attendants. If, however, the bride or groom is missing, wait as long as necessary or until one or the other calls off the wedding. If other significant family members, such as the parents or grandparents of the couple, have not arrived on time, convey that information to both the bride and groom (or have the wedding coordinator act as go-between) and facilitate their mutual decision on how long to wait before proceeding with the ceremony.

When Someone in the Wedding Party Faints

During the rehearsal, one key word of advice, especially to the men, is "Don't lock your knees." Everyone, when nervous, tends to sway a little. If one knee is slightly bent and slightly ahead of the other, slight swaying or shifting of weight is possible and easily dispels tension. If the knees are locked, however, no movement is possible except falling, and that's when one is more likely to tip over in a faint.

Also encourage the wedding party to watch out for one another when up front. One attendant catching another and easing him or her to the front pew or even to the floor is far less distracting and embarrassing than a loud crash. Knowing that they have a place to go (the front pew) if they begin to feel "woozy" can also prevent further problems.

If someone does faint, however, stop the proceedings, have the person attended to with as little embarrassment as possible, and then continue the service. Avoid referring to the incident as you go on, and don't make the victim feel even more ridiculous by making him or her the brunt of a joke.

When the Flower Girl or Ring Bearer Acts Up

Children are children. They have a lot of energy, and God did not equip them to stand still for thirty to sixty minutes at a time.

Expect them to be normally active, and make arrangements for them to either sit down where they are, go stand with a family member in the wedding party, or be seated with their parents or grandparents in the congregation. Some activity should also be tolerated and ignored when possible. After all, once they have come down the aisle, they essentially have done their job—unless, of course, the actual rings are still on the ring bearer's pillow. (The best man should make it his job to secure them in time for the giving of rings.)

Two types of children take part in weddings: those who are afraid of crowds and whose cowering is easily handled by loved ones nearby, and entertainers, children who love crowds, especially people who laugh at their antics. Should such antics become a problem, a pastor may as well stop, laugh with the congregation, and then help the child find a safe place out of the limelight.

When Someone Interrupts the Wedding

"If anyone knows any reason why this couple should not marry, let him speak now or forever hold his peace!" Immediately a jilted lover stood up and demanded that the wedding be stopped. The bride had promised to marry him!

Ninety-nine times out of a hundred, this could happen only in the movies. In fact, this question is rarely asked anymore in modern wedding services. Since wedding announcements are so public now and usually announced well in advance, ample time is given for concerns to be raised prior to the wedding day.

But never say "never." Should such an interruption take place or any other commotion major enough to distract everyone's attention, you may as well stop, deal with the interruption, and then proceed as appropriate. Should someone actually raise a legitimate concern, it would be better to delay the service until the truth can be uncovered than to proceed with the wedding, only to have it annulled shortly thereafter.

When a Ring Is Dropped

The combination of nervousness and passing something as small as a ring is an accident waiting to happen. Here are some suggestions for lowering the potential for this mishap.

Encourage the ring person(s), usually the best man and sometimes also the maid or matron of honor, to have the ring out and ready at least a few moments before they are needed. Prior preparation eliminates the need for haste, keeps the spotlight off the individual, and thereby reduces the risk of dropping the ring.

Another suggestion is for the ring person(s) to place the ring into the minister's palm. This is much easier than trying to grasp a small ring between the index finger and thumb when it is already being held that way by the bearer. It also avoids "Do you have it yet?" "No, do you?" and that disheartening tinkling sound as it hits the floor.

If a ring-bearer cushion is used and the real rings are actually on it, know what type of knot was used to secure them. A simple bow knot is best because it is easily released, either when the ring is needed or preferably by the best man just prior to it being needed.

Despite all practical precautions, accidents do still happen. If the ring is dropped, simply stop the proceedings, calmly find it, and then proceed, trying not to embarrass the guilty party.

When a Ring Is Missing

During the final part of the vows, the maid of honor begins to whisper that she has forgotten the groom's ring. It is back in the hotel, inaccessible. The quick-thinking minister has some alternatives. If you are married, remove your own ring and temporarily use it if it is at least close to a fit. Another option would be to quietly ask for one from someone in the wedding party. Even if the fit is not exact, the symbolic ceremony of the exchange of rings is still meaningful, and no one in the congregation need know that there is a problem. The key is to downplay the problem, avoid embarrassing the maid of honor for her forgetfulness, and proceed as smoothly as possible so that the preciousness of the moment is not lost.

When the Photographer Is Obnoxious

The moment is holy. The bride and groom are staring into each other's tear-glistened eyes, proclaiming their lifelong commitment, and a photographer steps between the pastor and the couple to take a picture. As the flash goes off, the beauty and sacredness of the moment are lost forever.

In our day of modern technology, this incident need never happen. The official photographer, if professional, will have a zoom lens and nonflash film, but discussing picture taking prior to the ceremony will enable both you and the photographer to do your jobs.

Before the ceremony begins, ask the congregation to refrain from taking flash pictures from the end of the processional to the beginning of the recessional. Your gentle request will ensure the worship context of marriage and also help the official photographer to proceed unhindered.

When the Candles Won't Light

The candle lighters have proceeded down the aisle smoothly and in proper formation. They begin lighting the candles in the candelabra slowly, trying to stay in step with each other. Suddenly one candle refuses to light. The candle lighter tries again and again, but he is still on the third candle when the other lighter finishes and leaves. How embarrassing.

This problem is nearly eliminated by the following practical suggestions. Light the candles during the final practice at the rehearsal, then extinguish them. A once-lit wick is much easier to relight in the wedding service. The rehearsal is also a good time to practice using the acolyte tool rented with the candelabra. (For less formal candle lighting, a small box of wooden matches is recommended.)

Encourage the candle lighters to check on each other's progress after lighting each candle. This way they can proceed together, with one waiting for the other, rather than moving ahead and putting pressure on the one who remains. If the candle still will not light after a reasonable attempt, encourage the candle lighter to pass over it and continue. The world will not end if one candle is not lit.

A similar strategy is effective for the symbolic unity candle lighting by the bride and groom. Practicing this pageantry at the rehearsal is helpful to all involved and makes the candles easier to light at the wedding.

When the Minister Skips a Part of the Ceremony

Nearing the end of the wedding sermon, the minister chanced to glance at the soloist and noted a look of horror on her face. Suddenly it hit like a ton of bricks. In the nervousness of the moment, the pastor had unwittingly omitted the special music and gone right on to the message. Now what?

Generally when this happens someone in the wedding party (or near the front) will whisper the omission to the pastor in time to reenter the element into the program. At this point of acknowledgment, the pastor can choose one of three options: (1) subtly stop the proceedings where appropriate, admit the omission, and incorporate it immediately; (2) reinsert the omission at another appropriate point in the service and proceed as if it were planned that way; or (3) elect to leave the overlooked element out. This latter option is the least desirable, given all the work that went into planning the wedding. Also, if the vows or the signing of the legal documents are omitted, the wedding is invalid. These are the legal essentials of the wedding and must not be skipped.

One way to avoid the blooper of omission is to use a clearly marked order of service. Another useful tool is the wedding rehearsal, which irons out details and helps lower nervousness, even in the minister.

Careful forethought and calm common sense will help greatly in reducing and coping with wedding bloopers. The above scenarios are just a few of the crazy things that can happen. Tighten your seatbelt and be ready to add your own experiences to the list.

{ 3 }
Wedding Resources

THIS CHAPTER CONTAINS a variety of specific wedding ceremony elements, raw materials if you will, rather than finished products. Included are suggestions for the ceremony introduction, opening prayer, presentation of the bride, ceremony music and Scripture, sermon and illustrations, vows, exchange of rings, declaration of marriage, prayer of dedication, signing of the register, lighting of the unity candles, Communion, and finally, introduction of the newlywed couple. Elements are presented separately to encourage ministers using this manual to develop their own ceremonies in collaboration with wedding couples. By having all these resources together in one place, and adding your own as you have opportunity, you will save much time in planning individual ceremonies.

This chapter is also available at the Judson Press website (see Preface, XVII), so you can download it onto your computer for your personal use. Each time you perform a wedding ceremony, choose from these resources what is most appropriate for your situation and make any necessary adaptations, just as I have done from sources I have used over the years. Organize it on your computer, and then print out your tailor-made ceremony, complete with the participants' names.

Introductions to the Ceremony

Formal Church Wedding

As a minister of Christ and a pastor of this church, I warmly welcome each of you to this sanctuary today. We have gathered here in God's presence to witness the marriage vows of _____ and _____ .

A wedding is that special occasion when a man and woman publicly proclaim their love and declare their commitment to each other.

For all of us it will mean sharing in a most intimate and love-filled moment in the lives of two people we know and appreciate.

For _____ and _____ it is the time of formally committing themselves to one another in a marriage relationship that is to last a lifetime.

For us as a congregation of witnesses, by our presence here, we accept responsibility for supporting _____ and _____ in this new relationship into which they are about to enter.

We are called to rejoice in their happiness, to be patient when their humanness causes them to make mistakes, to help them in times of trouble and stress, and to pray for them regularly.

_____ and _____ are both pleased and honored that you have responded to their invitation to share these happy and sacred moments with them. Because this is a ceremony of worship, they would request that you refrain from taking flash pictures from now until the recessional.

———∿∿∿———

Modified Formal Church Wedding

I welcome you to this holy moment in the lives of _____ and _____ as we witness their exchange of marriage vows, the precious beginning of a lifetime commitment.

It was God who established marriage, that man and woman might have lifelong companionship, that natural instincts and affections might be fulfilled in mutual love, that children might have the benefit of family life, and that society might rest on a firm foundation.

_____ and _____ , the moment you have been planning for and looking forward to has finally arrived. As your family and friends, we have assembled in this place of worship, at your invitation, to witness the public exchange of your vows of lifelong commitment to each other.

Today is not the destination, however, but rather the beginning of a lifelong journey of learning to love one another. It is before both the people gathered here and before God that you commit yourselves to begin this journey today.

As you travel on this journey, you will need God's supporting strength to bring you through. It is appropriate, therefore, that we pause right now and invite God's involvement in your lives, to help you carry out the commitments you are about to make.

———∿∿∿———

Informal Church Wedding

As a minister of Christ and as one of the pastors of this church, I welcome each of you to this sanctuary this afternoon. We gather here in God's presence to witness the joyous occasion of the marriage of _____ and _____ .

_____ and _____ , a very special moment in your lives is now before us. We stand at the threshold of the uniting of your two lives. Before, in weddings you attended, it was always someone else making the vows. This time it is you who are becoming one.

As your family and friends, we have gathered to offer our love and support to you in this sacred ceremony by witnessing the public exchange of your vows of lifelong commitment to each other. We promise to stand with you in the normal adjustments that need to come when two distinct lives are united into one lifestyle.

We desire to rejoice in your happiness, to be patient when you make mistakes, to help you in times of trouble, and to uphold you before our Almighty God in prayer. May you find us to be truly supportive whenever you need us.

As we reflect, our minds are filled with fond memories from having spent time with each of you. Thus we rejoice with you over the prospect of the two of you fully sharing life together. We especially thank our God for the gift of life and love that he has granted you, and we voice our confidence that as you allow him, God will join with you in the fulfillment of your hopes and dreams for married life.

Great as today will be, however, it is not, in itself, the destination. Rather, it is the beginning of a lifelong journey of learning to love each other. Thus it is before God and the people gathered here that you commit yourselves to begin this journey.

———

Outdoor Wedding (Couple Living Together)

As a minister of Christ, I welcome you to this beautiful outdoor setting to celebrate a very special day in the life of _____ and _____ .

We are gathered here in God's presence, amid the beauty of God's creation, to witness the exchange of this couple's marriage vows, a public declaration of the commitment that they have already shared with one another privately.

_____ and _____ , that very special moment that you have been waiting and planning for has finally arrived. The weather has cooperated, everything is beautifully arranged, and as your family and friends, we have gathered in response to your request, that we might witness the exchange of your vows of lifelong commitment to each other.

By our presence here, we accept responsibility for supporting you, _____ and _____ , in your married life together. We wish to celebrate your happy times, to be patient with you when your humanness causes you to make mistakes, to help you through times of trouble and stress, and to strongly support each of you through times of disappointment and misunderstanding. Most of all, we promise to regularly pray for you, to our Almighty God. May you find us truly supportive whenever you need us.

_____ and _____ , today is a very significant day for you, as before God and these witnesses you share vows of lifelong commitment to each other. Yet today is but a beginning, the start of a lifelong journey of learning to love each other.

We recognize that good marriages do not simply happen. Rather, they require the efforts of two people, each very committed to making it work. And these two also need a power beyond themselves, a strength to draw on that fills each with self-sacrificing love.

We find that source of love and strength in God, and so it is fitting to turn to the Lord now in prayer, inviting God's presence and participation in this relationship.

—⟨ᨆᨆᨆ⟩—

Home Wedding

_____ and _____ , we as your closest family and friends have gathered here to celebrate with you the exchange of your marriage vows.

A wedding is a joyous occasion that marks the beginning of a very special adventure called marriage. The institution of marriage was given by God himself, who in his great wisdom gave us such a commitment that the need for affection might be fulfilled in the context of committed, mutual love; that truth and holiness might be passed on from generation to generation through the family unit; and that society might have a firm foundation on which to rest and build.

And so, much more than simply gathering for a social occasion, by our presence here as your invited witnesses, we share in a significant crossroads of your history. We are here to support you in your decision to marry, and we desire to be here for you during the journey of learning to love one another that follows this new beginning. As the regular struggles and challenges of life come your way, may you find us faithfully here beside you offering support.

As you know, good marriages do not simply happen. They require the strong efforts of the couple seeking to make their marriage work. They require the support, encouragement, and guidance of a supportive community. And they require a power beyond mere human effort, the strength and support of Almighty God himself. Only God can give us true, self-sacrificing love so essential to living with one another's humanness. Let us turn to God now, inviting his blessing on and participation in the vows you are about to make.

———∽∾∾∾∽———

Theme-Oriented Wedding

_____ and _____ join me in welcoming each of you
to this celebration of their marriage commitment to one another. Thank you, in advance, for your commitment to them and
the supportive ministry you will provide as they learn to build
an enriching, fulfilling, lifelong relationship.

The theme _____ and _____ have chosen for their
wedding is "Becoming One with God and with Each Other."
The principle here is that by God's love we are able to love each
other, and as we grow closer and closer to God, we are able to
grow closer and closer to each other.

Let us honor God for making this couple's committed love
possible by recognizing God's presence and inviting God's ongoing involvement in the journey called marriage.

Opening Prayers

———∽∾∾∾∽———

Thanksgiving for Love

Thank you, God, for the gift of life, for family and friends, and
for the strong bond of love that exists between _____ and

_____ .

Thank you, Almighty God, that you are right here among us
now, hearing each word of commitment, reading each thought
and intention. Thank you that we can turn to you in faith and
ask that you not only witness this ceremony, but that you also
be involved, in an integral way, with the carrying out of these
vows made here today.

Thank you, God, that we can commit to you the very sacred moments that are to follow, and we pray with thanksgiving that your blessing and love will be an integral part of the lives of _____ and _____ in the years to come as they call upon you. With heartfelt gratefulness, we pray in the name of Jesus Christ our Lord. Amen.

━━━◦◦◦━━━

Enduring Love

Lord, we bow in your holy presence, with hearts full of worship and praise. You are a God of enduring love who shares that perfect love with us that we might love one another.

Thank you for the evidence of this enduring love in _____ and _____ . Thank you that this same love that has drawn them to you and to each other will sustain them in their married life as they tackle all of the challenges that will come their way. Your gift of love is a love that lasts, Father, and for this we praise you.

Continue to fill us with so great a love, and especially grant _____ and _____ this powerful, enduring love that it might equip them to fulfill the vows they make this day. In Jesus' name, Amen.

━━━◦◦◦━━━

Channels of Love

We stand in your presence, Heavenly Father, and thank you that it is because of your great love for us that we are able to love one another. Thank you that your love shines through both _____ and _____ .

Thank you that you will continue the work you have already begun in their lives. Truly make them channels of your love, both to others and especially to each other, throughout their new life together. We pray in the strong name of Jesus our Lord. Amen.

—————————

Committed Love

Thank you, dear God, for your commitment to love each of us. Thank you for creating us with the ability to receive and give love—love that is self-sacrificing, love that makes commitment between us as imperfect human beings possible. Thank you for the evidence of this love that we see in the lives of _____ and _____ . Thank you for these sacred moments as they publicly declare this love and pledge their commitment one to the other.

Thank you, too, Lord, for the committed love of family and friends. Thank you for those gathered here and for their willingness to come alongside _____ and _____ in this commitment called marriage. May we be faithful and supportive of them, as they build their marriage and live out the commitments made this day.

And thank you, loving God, for your precious presence here. Listen to the words spoken. Look to the intent of our hearts. Grant strength and wisdom to carry out the commitments made as often as _____ and _____ seek your face. We commit these sacred moments to you now, O Lord. In the strong name of Jesus we pray. Amen.

—————————

Supportive Love

Thank you, Almighty God, that you are present here among us right now. Hear these vows of commitment, we pray, and grant to _____ and _____ the strength to fulfill them throughout their lifetime together. Amen.

—⌐ᴕᴕᴕ⌐—

Concerned Love

Lord, we stand in your gracious presence with mixed emotions. We are concerned about the timing and wisdom of this choice to marry that _____ and _____ have made. We are concerned out of love, having already shared with them personally our reservations. Yet they are doing what they firmly believe is your will for their lives. Thus we come, too, in gracious faith, not to condemn, criticize, or question, but rather to offer our support and encouragement.

Grant us all strength, especially _____ and _____, to face all the normal adjustments and challenges that come as they learn to live together. We all need your grace, Lord. May we never be ones to stand back and then point fingers when the challenges come. Rather, may we give _____ and _____ the love and support they will need to grow through any difficulties they encounter.

Thank you, God of grace, for meeting us here in these precious moments. Thank you that we can count on you to faithfully respond as _____ and _____ call on you for strength to live these vows of commitment that they are about to make. In Jesus' name we pray. Amen.

Presentation of the Bride

—⌐ᴕᴕᴕ⌐—

Traditional

Pastor: Who gives this woman to be married to this man?
Father: I do.

———∾∾∾———

Contemporary

Pastor: Who presents _____ to be married to _____ ?
Parent: I do.
(Alternatively, the response may be given by both parents, a family representative, or the children of the bride. Their responses may be as follow:)
Responses: We do.
               Her mother and I do.
               Her family does.
               We, her children, do.

———∾∾∾———

Presentation of Bride and Groom

Pastor: Who presents these individuals to be given in marriage?
Parents: We, their parents, do.

(Alternatives comparable to those mentioned above in Option 2 are also applicable here. Other wedding resources offer additional ideas for modern modifications of this traditional element.)

Appropriate Ceremony Music
———∾∾∾———

Processional and recessional anthems are generally selected by the paid organist or pianist for the wedding, based on their own repertoire. Traditional favorites are "Jesu, Joy of Man's

Desiring," Purcell's "Trumpet Voluntaire," Pachabel's "Canon in D," and Mendhelson's "Wedding March." If desired, the pastor or the couple are welcome to make suggestions, but be sure to make such requests early on so the musician has ample time to obtain and learn an unfamiliar piece.

―――∾∾∾―――

Congregational Praise Hymns

"Great Is Thy Faithfulness"
"Joyful, Joyful We Adore Thee"
"Now Thank We All Our God"
"O Perfect Love"
"O the Deep, Deep Love of Jesus"
"Praise Ye the Lord"
"Savior, Like a Shepherd Lead Us"
"Standing on the Promises"
"This Is a Day of New Beginnings"
"Thy Presence, Lord, Brought Joy"
"Wedding Song" ("There Is Love")

―――∾∾∾―――

Congregational Praise Choruses

"Bind Us Together"
"Bless His Holy Name"
"Great Is the Lord"
"I Love You, Lord"
"Majesty"
"My Tribute"
"Surely the Presence of the Lord Is in This Place"
"This Is the Day"

Relevant Scripture Passages

———∽∾∾∾———

Old Testament Scriptures

Then God said, "Let us make humankind in our image, according to our likeness; and let them have dominion over the fish of the sea, and over the birds of the air, and over the cattle, and over all the wild animals of the earth, and over every creeping thing that creeps upon the earth."

> So God created humankind in his image,
> in the image of God he created them;
> male and female he created them.

God blessed them, and God said to them, "Be fruitful and multiply, and fill the earth and subdue it; and have dominion over the fish of the sea and over the birds of the air and over every living thing that moves upon the earth."

God saw everything that he had made, and indeed, it was very good.

—Genesis 1:26–28,31a, NRSV

———•———

Then the LORD God said, "It is not good that the man should be alone; I will make him a helper as his partner." So out of the ground the LORD God formed every animal of the field and every bird of the air, and brought them to the man to see what he would call them; and whatever the man called every living creature, that was its name. The man gave names to all cattle, and to the birds of the air, and to every animal of the field; but for the man there was not found a helper as his partner. So the LORD God caused a deep sleep to fall upon the man, and he slept; then he took one of his ribs and closed up its place with flesh. And the rib that the LORD God had taken from the man he made into a woman and brought her to the man. Then the man said,

"This at last is bone of my bones
and flesh of my flesh;
this one shall be called Woman,
for out of Man this one was taken."
Therefore a man leaves his father and his mother and clings
to his wife, and they become one flesh.

—Genesis 2:18–24, NRSV

But Ruth said, "Do not urge me to leave you or turn back from
following you; for where you go, I will go, and where you lodge,
I will lodge. Your people shall be my people, and your God, my
God. Where you die, I will die, and there I will be buried. Thus
may the Lord do to me, and worse, if anything but death parts
you and me"

—Ruth 1:16–17

He who finds a wife finds a good thing,
And obtains favor from the LORD.

—Proverbs 18:22

House and wealth are an inheritance from fathers,
But a prudent wife is from the LORD.

—Proverbs 19:14

An excellent wife, who can find?
For her worth is far above jewels.
The heart of her husband trusts in her,
And he will have no lack of gain.
She does him good and not evil
All the days of her life. . . .
She looks well to the ways of her household,
And does not eat the bread of idleness.
Her children rise up and bless her;

Her husband also, and he praises her, saying:
"Many daughters have done nobly,
But you excel them all."
Charm is deceitful and beauty is vain,
But a woman who fears the LORD,
    she shall be praised.

                    —Proverbs 31:10–12, 27–30

Two are better than one because they have a good return for their labor. For if either of them falls, the one will lift up his companion. But woe to the one who falls when there is not another to lift him up. Furthermore, if two lie down together they keep warm, but how can one be warm alone? And if one can overpower him who is alone, two can resist him. A cord of three strands is not quickly torn apart.

                    —Ecclesiastes 4:9–12

New Testament Scriptures

And some Pharisees came to [Jesus], testing Him, and saying, "Is it lawful for a man to divorce his wife for any cause at all?" And He answered and said, "Have you not read, that He who created them from the beginning made them male and female, and said, 'For this cause a man shall leave his father and mother, and shall cleave to his wife; and the two shall become one flesh'? Consequently they are no more two, but one flesh. What therefore God has joined together, let no man separate." They said to Him, "Why then did Moses command to give her a certificate and divorce her?" He said to them, "Because of your hardness of heart, Moses permitted you to divorce your wives; but from the beginning it has not been this way. And I say to you, whoever divorces his wife, except for immorality and marries another commits adultery."

—Matthew 19:3–9

Now concerning the things about which you wrote, it is good for a man not to touch a woman. But because of immoralities, let each man have his own wife, and let each woman have her own husband. Let the husband fulfill his duty to his wife, and likewise also the wife to her husband. The wife does not have authority over her own body, but the husband does; and likewise also the husband does not have authority over his own body, but the wife does. Stop depriving one another, except by agreement for a time that you may devote yourselves to prayer, and come together again lest Satan tempt you because of your lack of self-control.

—1 Corinthians 7:1–5

And be subject to one another in the fear of Christ.

Wives, be subject to you own husbands, as to the Lord. . . . Husbands, love your wives, just as Christ also loved the church and gave Himself up for her. . . . So husbands ought also to love their own wives as their own bodies. He who loves his own wife loves himself; for no one ever hated his own flesh, but nourishes and cherishes it, just as Christ also does the church.

—Ephesians 5:21–22,25,28–29

Love is patient, love is kind, and is not jealous, love does not brag and is not arrogant, does not act unbecomingly; it does not seek its own, is not provoked, does not take into account a wrong suffered, does not rejoice in unrighteousness, but rejoices with the truth; bears all things, believes all things, hopes all things, endures all things. Love never fails. . . . But now abide faith, hope, love, these three; but the greatest of these is love.

—1 Corinthians 13:4–8a,13

—◦◦◦—

Scripture Medley for Antiphonal Reading

Reader 1: Therefore, as God's chosen people, holy and dearly loved, clothe yourselves with compassion, kindness, humility, gentleness, and patience.

Reader 2: Bear with each other and forgive whatever grievances you may have against one another. Forgive as the Lord forgave you.

Reader 1: And over all these virtues put on love, which binds them all together in perfect unity. (Colossians 3:12–14)

Reader 2: There is faith, hope and love, these three; but the greatest of these is love (1 Corinthians 13:13).

Reader 1: "For I know the plans I have for you," declares the LORD. "Plans to prosper you and not harm you, plans to give you a future and a hope.

Reader 2: "Then you will call upon me and pray to me and I will listen to you. You will seek me and find me when you seek me with all your heart. I will be found by you," declares the LORD. (Jeremiah 29:11–14a)

Reader 1: And the two will become one flesh. So they are no longer two, but one (Mark 10:8).

Reader 2: Two are better than one because they have a good return for their work.

Reader 1: If one falls down, their friend can help them up. But pity the one who falls and has no one to help them up!

Reader 2: Also, if two lie down together, they will keep warm. But how can one keep warm alone?

Reader 1: Though one may be overpowered, two can defend themselves. A cord of three strands is not quickly broken. (Ecclesiastes 4:9–12, NIV adapted)

Reader 2: Place me like a seal over your heart, like a seal over your arm; for love is as strong as death . . . many waters cannot quench love; rivers cannot wash it away (Song of Solomon 8:6–7b).

Reader 1: Honor one another above yourselves. Never be lacking in zeal, but keep your spiritual fervor, serving the Lord.

Reader 2: Be joyful in hope, patient in affliction, faithful in prayer. (Romans 12:10b–12)

Reader 1: May the God of hope fill you with all joy and peace as you trust in him, so that you may overflow with hope by the power of the Holy Spirit (Romans 15:13, NIV).

Reader 2: May the God who gives endurance and encouragement give you a spirit of unity among yourselves as you follow Christ Jesus, so that with one heart and mouth you may glorify the God and Father of our Lord Jesus Christ (Romans 15:5–6, NIV).

———∽∾∾∾∾∽———

Alternative Meaningful Paraphrases

Out of respect for Christ, be courteously reverent to one another.

Wives, understand and support your husbands in ways that show your support for Christ. The husband provides leadership to his wife the way Christ does to his church, not by domineering but by cherishing. So just as the church submits to Christ as he exercises such leadership, wives should likewise submit to their husbands.

Husbands, go all out in your love for your wives, exactly as Christ did for the church—a love marked by giving, not getting. Christ's love makes the church whole. His words evoke her beauty. Everything he does and says is designed to bring the best out of her, dressing her in dazzling white silk, radiant with holiness. And that is how husbands ought to love their wives. They're really doing themselves a favor—since they're already "one" in marriage.

No one abuses his own body, does he? No, he feeds and pampers it. That's how Christ treats us, the church, since we are part of his body. And this is why a man leaves father and mother and cherishes his wife. No longer two, they become "one flesh." This is a huge mystery, and I don't pretend to understand it all. What is clearest to me is the way Christ treats the church. And this provides a good picture of how each husband is to treat his wife, loving himself in loving her, and how each wife is to honor her husband.

—Ephesians 5:21–33, THE MESSAGE

If I speak with human eloquence and angelic ecstasy but don't love, I'm nothing but the creaking of a rusty gate. If I speak God's Word with power, revealing all his mysteries and making everything plain as day, and if I have faith that says to a mountain, "Jump," and it jumps, but I don't love, I'm nothing.

If I give everything I own to the poor and even go to the stake to be burned as a martyr, but I don't love, I've gotten nowhere. So, no matter what I say, what I believe, and what I do, I'm bankrupt without love.

Love never gives up.
Love cares more for others than for self.
Love doesn't want what it doesn't have.
Love doesn't strut,
Doesn't have a swelled head,
Doesn't force itself on others,
Isn't always "me first,"
Doesn't fly off the handle,
Doesn't keep score of the sins of others,
Doesn't revel when others grovel,
Takes pleasure in the flowering of truth,
Puts up with anything,
Trusts God always,
Always looks for the best,
Never looks back,

But keeps going to the end.
Love never dies.

—1 Corinthians 13:1–8a, THE MESSAGE

———•———

(In the following paraphrase, insert the couple's names where the word love is used.)

_____ and _____ are patient, _____ and _____ are kind, and are not jealous, _____ and _____ do not brag and are not arrogant, _____ and _____ do not act unbecomingly; they do not seek their own, are not provoked, do not take into account a wrong suffered, do not rejoice in unrighteousness, but rejoice with the truth; _____ and _____ bear all things, believe all things, hope all things, endure all things. _____ and _____'s love never fails.... But now abide faith, hope, love, these three; but the greatest of these is love.

—1 Corinthians 13:4–8a,13, adapted

———•———

The same goes for you wives: Be good wives to your husbands, responsive to their needs.... What matters is not your outer appearance—the styling of your hair, the jewelry you wear, the cut of your clothes—but your inner disposition.

Cultivate inner beauty, the gentle, gracious kind that God delights in. The holy women of old were beautiful before God that way, and were good, loyal wives to their husbands....

The same goes for you husbands: Be good husbands to your wives. Honor them, delight in them. As women they lack some of your advantages. But in the new life of God's grace, you're equals. Treat your wives, then, as equals so your prayers don't run aground.

—1 Peter 3:1a,3–5,7, THE MESSAGE

Sermon Outlines

For the Traditional Wedding of a Christian Couple: Ephesians 5:21–33

I. Be subject to one another in the fear of Christ (v. 21).

    A. Mutual subjection.

    B. By personal choice (I submit myself to you).

    C. Out of reverence for God.

II. Wives, respect your husbands (vv. 22–24).

    A. Love comes more naturally.

    B. Respect takes work.

    C. Respect is offered, not earned.

III. Husbands, love your wives unconditionally (v. 25).

    A. Love needs to overcome self-centeredness.

    B. Love needs to be for her alone.

    C. Love is offered unconditionally, not earned.

For the God-seeking Couple: 1 Corinthians 13

I. What you put into your marriage is what you will get out of it.

    A. Good marriages do not just happen.

    B. It takes both partners to create a good marriage.

II. Love needs to be expressed in caring.

    A. Glowing performance is not enough (vv. 1–4).

    B. Practical caring puts a handle on love.

III. Use the mighty resources of God available to you.

    A. On our own, we cannot truly love.

    B. God's strength is greater than our own.

    C. Only in God's strength can we begin to live (vv. 4–8a).

For the Nominal or Non-Christian Couple: Genesis 2:18–24

I.   Include God meaningfully in your marriage.
   A. God provided marriage to meet our need.
   B. God gave away the first bride.
II. Study the instruction manual.
   A. The Bible is the book God wrote for us.
   B. It teaches how to have good relationships.
III. Live what you learn.
   A. Let what you learn enrich your marriage.
   B. Begin with yourself.

Scripture Medley

If a medley of Scriptures is preferred to one text, share the following principles.

I.   Marriage is God's idea (Genesis 2:18–25).
II. A lifelong relationship in marriage is God's ideal (Matthew 19:8–9).
III. Self-giving love in marriage is God's investment (1 Corinthians 13:4–8a).

Suggested Illustrations

Commitment

A pig and a chicken were overheard discussing what the farmer was planning to have for breakfast the next morning. The chicken, quite sure of her information, said that the farmer was to have bacon and eggs the next morning. At this news the pig began to cry. Startled, the chicken asked, "Whatever is the matter with you?" To which the pig replied, "For you giving to the breakfast is merely a contribution. For me it is total commitment." Marriage is total commitment.

———∽∾∾∽———

Triangle

If you choose to include God meaningfully in your new married life, think in terms of a triangle. If we see God at the top point and the bride and groom side by side as its base, we see that as the bride and groom each individually draw closer to God, they also automatically draw closer to each other (moving up the triangle). This is a helpful picture to keep in mind. One of the best things we can do for our marriage is to improve our relationship to God.

God

bride   groom

———∽∾∾∽———

Read the Directions

Marriage was God's idea, and the Lord gave us an instruction manual to keep this sacred union strong. It is called the Bible. This guide is full of excellent ideas on how to build solid personal relationships, be they friendships, family relationships, or marriage. Do not wait until all else fails to read the instructions. Rather, read these pages often and draw on their wisdom. Grow closer to God and to each other through living out his word of counsel.

Vows

———∽∾∾∽———

While some couples prefer to write their own vows, others prefer to modify ones drawn from several sources. Still others will simply choose a set of vows already written. Giving a couple a variety of choices helps them claim ownership to the commitment they will make. Make up a handout of a variety of vow options for couples making choices. Some are provided below, and others can be found in Appendix G.

————◦◦◦◦————

Traditional

In preparation for your vows, I invite you to face each other and join hands.

The Charge

Pastor: _____ *(groom)*, wilt thou have this woman to be thy wedded wife, to live together after God's ordinance, in the holy estate of matrimony? Wilt thou love her, comfort her, honor and keep her, in sickness and in health, and, forsaking all others, keep thee only unto her so long as you both shall live?
Groom: I will.
Pastor: _____ *(bride)*, wilt thou have this man to be thy wedded husband, to live together after God's ordinance, in the holy estate of matrimony? Wilt thou love him, comfort him, honor and keep him, in sickness and in health, and, forsaking all others, keep thee only unto him so long as you both shall live?
Bride: I will.

The Vows (Groom first; then bride)

Repeat after me:

I, _____, do take thee, _____, to be my lawful wedded wife; to have and to hold from this day forward, for better, for worse, for richer for poorer, in sickness and in health, to love and to cherish till death us do part and thereto I plight thee my troth.

Repeat after me:

I, _____, do take thee, _____, to be my lawful wedded husband; to have and to hold from this day forward, for better, for worse, for richer for poorer, in sickness and in health, to love and to cherish till death us do part and thereto I plight thee my troth.

———∽∽∽———

Updated Traditional

As an expression of your willingness to totally commit yourself to one another, I invite you to face each other and join hands.

The Charge
Pastor: _____ *(groom)*, will you have _____ (bride) to be your wife, to live together after God's ordinance in the holy estate of matrimony? Will you love her, comfort her, honor and keep her in sickness and in health, and, forsaking all others, keep yourself only for her so long as you both shall live?
Groom: I do.
Pastor: _____ *(bride)*, will you have _____ (groom) to be your husband, to live together after God's ordinance in the holy estate of matrimony? Will you love him, comfort him, honor and keep him in sickness and in health, and, forsaking all others, keep yourself only for him so long as you both shall live?
Bride: I do.

The Vows (Groom first; then bride)
As a further sign of your heartfelt desire, I invite you to repeat these words after me:

In the presence of God, and before these witnesses, I, _____, take you _____, to be my wife, to have and to hold from this day forward, for better, for worse; for richer, for poorer; in sickness and in health; in joy and in sorrow; to love and to cherish and to be faithful to you alone, as long as we both shall live.

As a further sign of your heartfelt desire, I invite you to repeat these words after me:

In the presence of God, and before these witnesses, I, _____, take you _____, to be my husband, to have and to hold from this day forward, for better, for worse; for richer, for poorer; in sickness and in health; in joy and in sorrow; to love and to cherish and to be faithful to you alone, as long as we both shall live.

———∽∾∾∾∾∾———

Contemporary

For the giving of your vows of commitment, I invite you now to face each other and join hands.

The Charge

Pastor: _____ *(groom)*, do you purpose to live with _____ *(bride)* in a fashion consistent with God's design for marriage? Do you purpose to love her, honor her, and be faithful to her in times of personal need and personal blessing? Do you pledge, with God's help and to the best of your ability, to seek to establish and maintain honest, open, and loving communication between yourself and _____ *(bride)*? Forsaking all others, do you promise to remain faithful to _____ *(bride)* as long as you both shall live?

Groom: I do.

Pastor: _____ *(bride)*, do you purpose to live with _____ *(groom)* in a fashion consistent with God's design for marriage? Do you purpose to love him, honor him, and be faithful to him in times of personal need and personal blessing? Do you pledge, with God's help and to the best of your ability, to seek to establish and maintain honest, open, and loving communication between yourself and _____ *(groom)*?

Forsaking all others, do you promise to remain faithful to
_____ *(groom)* as long as you both shall live?
Bride: I do.

The Vows (Groom first; then bride)

As a further sign of your lifelong commitment to one another,
and of your desire to fully participate in both the privileges and
the obligations of married life, I invite you to declare your promise to one another.

_____ *(groom)*, repeat after me:

In the presence of God, and before our witnesses and friends,
_____ *(groom's name)*, with joy and in love, I take you to
be my wife, to be the mother of my children, and the companion of my days. I promise to fully share my life with you,
through days of happiness or sadness, abundance or want. I
pledge to you my unfailing love always.

_____ *(bride)*, repeat after me:

In the presence of God, and before our witnesses and friends,
_____ *(bride's name)*, with joy and in love, I take you to
be my husband, to be the father of my children, and the companion of my days. I promise to fully share my life with you,
through days of happiness or sadness, abundance or want. I
pledge to you my unfailing love always.

Exchange of Rings

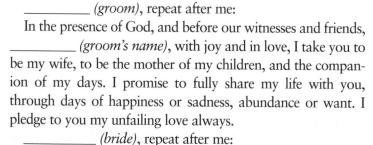

Hint: In the exchanging of the rings, avoid the blooper of
dropped rings by transferring the wedding bands from an open
palm, not from fingertips to fingertips. Thus, the honor attendants should place the rings in the open palm of the bride and
groom, and if the couple surrenders the rings to the pastor for a

blessing before the exchange, they too should place the rings in the pastor's open palm.

———✦✦✦———

Traditional

(Pastor speaks to the bride and groom in turn, starting first with the groom.)
Pastor: What token do you give as a symbol of your faithfulness?
Response: A ring.
(Take ring from honor attendant.)
Pastor: Repeat after me as you place a ring on the other's finger:
This ring I give thee in token of the covenant made this day between us. In the name of the Father, and of the Son, and of the Holy Spirit. Amen.

———✦✦✦———

Contemporary 1

Pastor: What physical sign do you give that symbolizes the vows you have made to one another?
Couple: Rings.
(Receive rings from honor attendants.)
Pastor: Repeat after me as you place a ring on the other's finger: *(Groom first; then bride)*
I give you this ring that you may wear it as a symbol of the vows I have made to you today.

———✦✦✦———

Contemporary 2

Pastor: What outward and visible sign do you give that symbolizes the vows you have made to one another?

Couple: Rings.

(Minister collects rings.)

Pastor: May these beautiful golden rings symbolize the purity and never-ending love you each have for your chosen companion in life.

Pastor: Repeat after me as you place a ring on the other's finger: *(Groom first; then bride)*

I give you this ring, that you may wear it as a symbol of our constant faith and abiding love.

Declaration of Marriage

Traditional

Those whom God hath joined together, let no one put asunder. For as much as _____ and _____ have consented together in holy wedlock, and have witnessed the same before God and this company, and thereto have given and pledged their troth either to other, and have declared the same by giving and receiving of a ring, and by joining of hands; I pronounce that they be husband and wife together, in the name of the Father, and of the Son, and of the Holy Ghost. Amen. *(Invite the couple to kiss.)*

Modified Traditional

For as much as _____ and _____ have promised to be faithful and true to each other, and have witnessed the same, before God and this gathering, by spoken vows and by giving and receiving rings in pledge, they enter now into a new estate. As a minister of Jesus Christ, I pronounce them husband and wife. What God has joined together, let no one put asunder. *(Invite the couple to kiss.)*

———∽∽∽———

Contemporary

For as much as _____ and _____ have made this solemn covenant of marriage before God and this company, I declare them to be husband and wife, in the name of the Father, and of the Son, and of the Holy Spirit. Amen. *(Invite the couple to kiss.)*

Prayer of Dedication

———∽∽∽———

Traditional

(Invite the couple to kneel.)

O eternal God, creator and sustainer of all humankind, giver of all spiritual grace, and author of everlasting life, send thy blessing upon these thy servants, this man and this woman, whom we bless in thy name; that they, living faithfully together, may surely perform and keep the vow and covenant between them made (whereof this ring given and received is a token and pledge) and may ever remain in perfect love and peace together and live according to thy laws.

O God, who hast so consecrated the state of matrimony that in it is represented the spiritual marriage and unity betwixt Christ and his church, look mercifully upon these thy servants, that they may love, honor, and cherish each other, and so live together in faithfulness and patience, in wisdom and true godliness, that their home may be a haven of blessing and of peace.

God the Father, God the Son, God the Holy Ghost bless, preserve, and keep you: the Lord mercifully with his favor look upon you and fill you with all spiritual benediction and grace that ye may so live in this life that in the world to come ye may have life everlasting through Jesus Christ our Lord. Amen.

Contemporary 1

(Invite the couple to kneel.)

Thank you, Father, for this happy occasion that we celebrate. Thank you for giving us love and marriage. Thank you for the gift of husband and wife.

(Place hand on groom's shoulder or head.) We ask that you bless _____. Make him the husband you want him to be by your mighty power working within him.

(Place hand on bride's shoulder or head.) Bless also _____. Make her a fitting wife and companion for _____. Lead her to full potential through your mighty power working within her.

Bless them together as a couple as they begin this lifelong journey called marriage. Grant them the necessary grace to live out the vows they have made this day.

And help us as their family and friends to support and encourage them in this new life together.

Father, we commit both ourselves and this couple to you now in solemn dedication. May the grace of our Lord Jesus Christ, the love of God, and the communion of the Holy Spirit be with you all. Amen.

---ᴀᴏᴏᴀ---

Contemporary 2

(Invite the couple to kneel.)

Father, we worship you for the precious gift of love that enables us to love one another and even commit our very lives to each other. Thank you that your love flows within _____ and _____. Thank you that they have declared this love to the world by publicly committing themselves to one another in an exclusive, lifelong love relationship.

Grant them your ongoing grace and love to fulfill these vows daily. Grant them strength when the struggles of life seek to burst their love cocoon. Grant them understanding when expectations remain unmet and they express their innermost feelings of loss to one another. Help them work out these normal difficulties of life, and may these challenges cause their marriage ties to grow stronger and stronger.

Lord, we commit _____ and _____ to you now in these sacred moments. Grant that they may achieve all that you have created and called them to be. In the strong name of Jesus, our Lord, we pray. Amen.

Signing of the Register
(Canadian Ceremonies Only)

---ᴀᴏᴏᴀ---

Part of the legal process of verifying marriage is the signing of several documents. Historically in Canada, clergy were seen as an agent for the government. When they obtained their "clergy number," they were given a supply of government documents to be used for registering any weddings they performed.

Over time the Canadian system has graduated more toward the American system, in which most of the official documentation is filled out at the local courthouse with the individual responsible for issuing marriage licenses. Currently the pastor has forms to fill out and file with the Department of Vital Statistics that the wedding did take place as planned. Most churches also provide a certificate of marriage signed by the pastor so that the couple has some immediate legal proof of their marriage until their official certificate of marriage arrives in the mail. (This must be prepaid and ordered when the marriage license is obtained.)

During the evolution of this process, Canadians developed a tradition of including the signing of wedding documentation during the ceremony itself. This drama of legalizing the marriage by signing papers usually occurred after the dedication prayer, solemnizing the marriage. The couple themselves signed first, the bride using her maiden name for the last time, and then the maid of honor and best man signed as witnesses. Finally, the pastor signed the document declaring that he or she had performed the ceremony and included his or her clergy number. Usually all this was done while special music was sung or played.

For those Canadian ceremonies continuing this tradition, here are some suggestions.

———✿✿✿———

Public Signing

A small table is prearranged on the platform, with the documents and a working pen placed on a suitable writing surface. (Lace tablecloths require more paper to cushion the document.) A chair is also provided. The bride is seated and signs first. The groom may simply lean past the bride to sign, while she remains seated. Then this pattern is followed by the maid or matron of honor, who is seated, and the best man, both of whom sign as witnesses to the document. The pastor then takes his or her turn at signing. It is the pastor's responsibility to know where each person is to sign and to direct the writers accordingly. Witnesses will need to include their addresses.

Alternatively, the couple may choose to omit the chair and seating of the signers. In this arrangement, all parties simply lean forward at the table to sign the documents when it is their turn.

Private Signing

Some couples choose to leave the platform and sanctuary during a special musical number and sign the necessary papers in an adjoining classroom or office. The pastor and honor attendants need to accompany them. All return to the platform for the conclusion of the ceremony.

Unity Candle Ceremony

Some couples choose to include in their ceremony a symbolic drama of lighting a unity candle, depicting the change in their status from two individual lives to a combined life. The paradox, of course, is that now both exist: their individual lives continue, but a new oneness is added.

Traditional Ceremony: Three Candles

Typically, a small table is set on the platform, centrally or to one side, on which two single tapers are placed on either side of a larger pillar candle. The tapers represent the individual lives of the bride and groom. Usually after the vows have been spoken and the rings are exchanged, the couple walks together to the table where the taper candles are already burning. The bride and groom each take a taper in hand and join the flames from the tapers to light the center candle, the so-called unity candle. As this drama is being enacted, the pastor may explain to the congregation the symbolic significance of two lives becoming one, as represented by the candle ceremony. Alternatively (or additionally), the couple may choose to have instrumental or vocal special music play during this time.

The following are some suggestions for and variations of this optional service element.

Who Lights the Tapers?

1. The taper candles are lit by the candle lighters when the candelabra are lit at the beginning of the service.

2. The tapers are lit by the mothers (or parents) of the bride and groom, after the seating of the parents and before the entry of the bridal party. This option symbolizes the families from which the couple have drawn their gift of life.

3. The bride and groom light their own candles as part of the unity candle ceremony, after the vows have been said and the rings have been exchanged.

What to Do with the Tapers?

1. After lighting the unity candle, the couple extinguish their own tapers, signifying their choice to make the marriage relationship their primary focus.

2. The couple return their tapers to their holders, leaving them lit, representing two individual lives continuing, yet making the choice regularly to live in unity and to fulfill their marriage vows.

———ᔔᔔ———

Another Option: Four Candles

In this variation on the traditional unity candle ceremony, there are four candles arranged on the table in a diamond format: two representing the bride and groom (left and right), one representing their married life together (front or bottom), and the fourth representing Christ (back or top). (A small cross placed behind the Christ candle is also appropriate.) In this arrangement only the Christ candle has been lit previously by the candle lighters.

As the newlyweds go to the table, they each remove their unlit tapers from the holders and light them from the Christ candle. The minister explains that this symbolizes that each has drawn life and breath from God. The couple then lights the unity candle, depicting the unity in which they will strive to live. Their candles are then returned to their places, either lit or unlit, with the appropriate explanation mentioned above.

Communion

———ᔔᔔ———

Another way some couples choose to symbolize their new marital unity, as well as their spiritual union, is to participate in the Lord's Supper at or near the conclusion of the wedding ceremony. When this drama is part of the service a small table is preset with the elements arranged for the couple. Normally only the couple participates in this sacred symbolism, but the honor attendants or even the entire bridal party may be included as well. The following format could be used as a guide for either setting.

————〜⌀⌀⌀⌀————

The Couple and/or Wedding Party

Following the dedication prayer, the minister invites the couple to the table of our Lord with words such as the following:

As you begin a new life together in marriage, may you also renew your spiritual commitment by expressing your unity with Christ. The table of our Lord is for sinners such as us, who come in sincerity and humbleness, confessing our sinfulness and expressing the desire to live more faithfully for God in the days ahead. It is fitting then to express your commitment to God as well as to each other by now taking your first Communion together as husband and wife. Let us take a moment now to personally prepare to participate at the Lord's table.

After an appropriate pause, extend the bread to the couple, declaring, "This is Christ's body, broken for you." After they eat the element, extend the cup (individual or common cup) with the words, "This represents Christ's blood, shed for the forgiveness of your sins." Conclude with a brief prayer of thanksgiving for Christ's great sacrifice of love on our behalf.

Some minor modifications of the introductory comments and practical serving of the Communion bread and wine would be necessary if the couple wants to include the honor attendants or entire wedding party in partaking of the elements.

————〜⌀⌀⌀⌀————

Entire Congregation

In some traditions, the entire congregation participates in the Communion service. Even couples outside such traditions may like to choose this option. In such cases, arrangements need to be made for serving the congregation. The couple should consider whether the guests will be invited to come forward to the altar rail or if individual servings will be passed through the congregation while the guests remain seated. Be sure that you are familiar with the church's guidelines concerning the administering of Communion. Some denominations allow only certain persons (e.g., ordained ministers, deacons, ushers) to serve the Communion elements.

Introduction of the Newlywed Couple

Given our current societal views, the minister is wise not to assume that the couple wishes to be traditionally introduced as "Mr. and Mrs. Harry Smith." This traditional pronouncement may be chosen by the couple during the wedding planning, but other choices should be offered as well. (See chapter 2 and Appendix E.) Make every effort to use what the couple has chosen to be their legal married name in your introduction of them to the congregation. This choice is normally made when the couple fills out the legal forms to obtain their marriage license at the courthouse, although in some states, the decision is not finalized until the couple signs the license itself after the wedding is over.

PART II

Funerals

{ 4 }

Funeral Ethics

As the pastor, the only staff member of the small church, approached yet another funeral, a great sense of fatigue and frustration settled upon her. The busyness all started on Saturday with a wedding, which made it seem as if she had had two Sundays in one weekend. Then there were the two services on Sunday, making for a full day, plus visiting with the grieving family. Now, today, supposedly her day off, the funeral message and service awaited development. With no staff member with whom to share the load, the pastor trudged to her office, trying to psyche herself up for quality ministry, while inside she felt like escaping to freedom from this constant demand for giving. Needs, needs, needs! If it were not for her clear sense of calling. . . .

MINISTRY IS ALWAYS CHALLENGING because of its many faces. Shifting gears from weddings, to church services, to funerals—not to mention personal needs, family needs, other church people's needs—stresses and stretches even good flexibility. Such pressure also greatly tempts the minister to cut corners in preparation, cut back on ministry to the grieving, and cut across boundaries that are normally respected. Any minister must work hard at seeking to balance these many needs and maintain appropriate boundaries. Pastors are called by God to a high ethical standard, even in the face of fatigue from dueling with the competing needs of ministry.

While pastors are struggling with our own issues, ministry is begging to happen within the context of a death. Death is never convenient for anyone, the pastor included. Yet death deserves to be given immediate attention. It is a sacred time, inviting the highest of ethical standards and pastoral care.

A key word that describes people in grief is vulnerability. When we experience a deep loss, like the death of a loved one, our sense of reality is altered for a time, and we become extremely susceptible to the influence of those around us. For a time we even desire that others simply tell us what to do so that we can essentially function without thinking. Since the time of grief leaves most people vulnerable, it is extremely important that authority figures in their lives respond from the highest possible ethical standards of honesty and truth. This importance certainly includes funeral directors, as our laws seek to address. But it also includes ministers, who are allowed to be a "law unto themselves."

A Theology of Death and Dying

Increasingly important and providing a solid foundation for high ethical standards surrounding funerals is an adequate theology of death and dying. How do you as a minister view death? Is it something to "get past" as quickly as possible, like our society often tries to do? (In the "olden days," bodies were washed at home and laid in state for a day or more. Now bodies are removed as quickly as possible from our sight.) If "out of sight" is our mind-set, funerals will be a necessary evil—something to be endured and "gotten over with" as quickly as possible.

Or do you see death as a normal part of the life cycle? God did not create our bodies to last forever, nor to be indestructible. Can you help people prepare for this final stage of life before, during, and after it touches their family? Do you preach enough on heaven and on viewing life now in the perspective of eternity? Can you allow people the necessary time to grieve, even though it is painful for everyone?

And then, more specifically with regard to ethics, do you see the timing of death as something people have a right to choose, or is it only for God to choose? Increasingly this is becoming an issue today, as assisted suicide becomes more evident in the foreground, while in the background some elderly people quietly give up on life and seek to end it by discontinuing eating. What will we teach survivors attending these funerals, concerning the giver and taker of life?

An adequate theology of death and dying is ever growing and developing. It is dynamic as it matures, ever grappling with finding the appropriate balance between these four areas: the nature of life and death; death as friend and foe; death choices; and life after death. Your theology of death and dying will directly impact how you respond to these issues in your ministry and will color how you conduct a funeral. Which of the following areas do you need to work on, to better round out your own theology of death and dying?

The Nature of Life and Death

Your theology of the nature of life and death will directly impact how you conduct a funeral. For example, if you major on death as the reigning power or consequence of sin (Romans 5:12–14; 6:23; 1 Corinthians 15:56; James 1:15), gloom and punishment will tend to be the theme of your service. Since this spirit is uncomfortable for everyone, the goal will be to "get through the service as quickly as possible and put it behind us." Simply trying to "get past death" and "get back to normal" greatly hinders the grief process and stifles our Christian hope.

At the other extreme are those who major on the life side, downplaying the death and focusing exclusively on the new life already gained. This is the "no pain (sting) in death" side (Isaiah 25:8; Hosea 13:14; 1 Corinthians 15:54–55; Philippians 1:21–23). This theology refuses to embrace the pain of the dying process and the resulting loss. This funeral will tend to try to be uplifting only. Tears have no place here. We must be joyful. The deceased is in a better place (unless everyone knows he or she "went the other way," in which case this theology and this funeral are in a dilemma).

A healthier balance between these two extremes is to recognize life and death as a gift from God. God did not make our bodies to last forever. They wear out. They do not withstand aging, severe trauma, or casualty. Life and death are normal parts of the life cycle (Genesis 3:19; Psalm 90:3–6; Ecclesiastes 3:1–2; 12:7; Hebrews 9:27), although sometimes circumstances greatly speed up the "normal" part. To be sure, some deaths simply do not make sense. At these times let us help the grieving cling to the God of love in the midst of pain rather than trying to explain and justify God's unexpected action and timing.

A healthy emerging and developing theology of death and dying finds tears, laughter, and silence all to be appropriate and encouraged at the funeral. Such theology allows hope and grief to mingle. It views death as a sacred moment of pain, the beginning of healing.

Death as Friend and Foe

Another frame from which to articulate your theology of death is to hold in creative tension death as friend and foe. A theology of death solely as friend makes for a dangerous situation when conducting a funeral service. If you extol only how wonderful and freeing death is, you may inadvertently move someone toward suicide, so that they too are able to enjoy sweet release from the trials of life.

On the other hand, death strictly as foe invites us to avoid the topic of death and dying at all costs. An example of this view is people who see all talk of death as morbid and to be avoided entirely.

Seek a healthy balance here. Death is both friend, our final graduation to a whole new life, and foe, a painful wrenching from the known to the unknown, leaving behind a sense of loss. Both sides of this tension require exposure in a well-conducted funeral.

Death Choices

God's timing of death, as it intersects our stewardship of life, has encountered a new twist from modern technology, one that particularly challenges our theology of dying. For example, if God chooses when someone dies, how long do we overrule natural death and prolong existence of a body artificially through life-support equipment? When do we pull the plug? What never was an option before now appears to make the family, rather than God, choose when a loved one will die. What pastoral care and advice will you offer these struggling families, as you walk with them through making these tough choices? Will you encourage prolonging the death process or will you help them say good-bye to their loved one?

It is naturally within us to cling to life as long as possible. We are to be good stewards of the life given us by God and not shorten it by abusing our body, taking foolish risks, or snuffing out this precious gift of life. But when does physical existence stop being life? When is it God's will to let our loved one go? And, conversely, what of those who desire the "right" to choose their own termination? The theological tension here concerns at what point either desire becomes "playing God."

In addition to wrestling with this tough question, an equally difficult practical question arises. How will you minister to those within your pastoral care who choose a different theology than your own on this issue? Ministry remains your calling even in the face of a variety of death choices. While funerals are not the best avenue for theological debate, some teaching and influence will naturally emerge from you, based on your view of death choices, as you conduct funerals and minister to the grieving. How intentional will you be in this process?

Life after Death

What form does life take beyond the grave? From a theological perspective, several answers emerge, and each wields its own influence on the conducting of a funeral service. For example, there is the view of "soul sleep," the theological position that all souls enter a "limbo" state after physical death and remain in this mysterious vacuum until judgment day at Christ's return. If this view is your personal belief, your funeral message will tend to be quite nebulous regarding the afterlife of the deceased. This view greatly limits the Christian hope and comfort we can have by knowing our loved one is in Christ's presence. On the other hand, this position may be helpful when the deceased was not a Christian.

A secular adaptation of the "soul sleep" perspective is the idea that death is the ultimate end of life, with nothing beyond the grave. This view removes hope from the funeral service, both of life with Christ eternally and of any ultimate meaning to life here on earth. If we simply live to die, we are no different than the rest of creation.

Another highly theological view of life after death is the idea that a soul passes directly to heaven, or hell, at the time of physical death. Variations of this concept produce a surprising array of funeral purposes. For some the funeral is the time to "preach the deceased's soul to heaven." For others it is the time to condemn this obvious sinner to hell. Both of these judgmental purposes place the minister into a "playing God" role, a place God does not intend us to be. God decides who goes where. Only God is able to judge accurately and justly.

A healthier perspective of life and death allows for some mystery and provides a great deal of both hope and meaning to life. The mystery involves no simple answer to the life after death issue. Christ said to the thief on the cross, "Truly I say to you, today you shall be with Me in Paradise" (Luke 23:43). Where is this paradise? We do not know exactly, but it is enough to know that we are with Christ. Preaching that the believing loved one is in Christ's presence fits within the meaning of this text and brings great comfort and hope to the grieving family. Even when the spiritual condition of the individual is unclear or unknown, we can trust God for a just response. God alone truly knows the deceased's final response to God's offer of love. Allowing for some mystery, then, and allowing God to be God are both important to an adequate theology of death and dying.

Our great Christian hope is based on this present life being temporary, with everlasting life beyond the grave as our true goal and purpose for existence. This theme helps us approach death and dying, not so much as facing the inescapable grim reaper, but rather as experiencing a final, though painful, graduation to a much greater life. This theology gives meaning to life on this earth and provides hope that is not destroyed even by earthly cessation of human life. It provides room for the lingering, graceful acceptance of the natural exchange of our present life form for another. But such hope must not be allowed to snuff out pain and grief. Both sides, hope and pain, are essential to a healthy grieving process. Both are to be invited to, and expressed in, the funeral service.

How does your theology of death and dying deal with the issues surrounding the nature of life and death, death as friend and foe, death choices, and life after death? How will you walk through the stages of death with your people? Certainly, as you do, unresolved issues in your own theology of death will be exposed. How will you grow through these experiences? How will you teach your people to face death? Your own theology of death, as it emerges in your funeral services, will cast quite an influence. How healthy is this influence?

For additional study options and resources on developing a theology of death and dying, see the annotated bibliography.

Ethical Choices

In addition to the need for developing an adequate theology of death and dying, you are faced with other ethical issues surrounding the funeral itself. Just as we considered some of the ethical choices surrounding wedding scenarios in part I, we will now explore ethical issues that arise in the context of funerals, applying the same four ethical principles presented in the introduction of this manual:

- How can I be true to God and to the Scriptures?
- How can I be true to myself and my calling?
- How can I be true to the church I am serving?
- How can I be true to the individuals involved?

Funerals provide ministers with a wide array of ethical challenges and choices. The rest of this chapter offers an eclectic collection of dilemmas for your consideration.

"Doing" the Funeral
"Tailor-made" versus "One-Size-Fits-All" Funerals

You may be tempted to just pull out "the old manual," change the name, and simply "do" a funeral. You may even seek to justify this technique by saying, "No one listens to these things anyway," and "I am so terribly busy I just have to cut corners this time." Temptation is real. Lack of time is real. But you are a minister of Christ and thus are called to minister according to individual need, just as Christ did. You must be true to yourself and your calling.

How can you do this? One special way is to fit the funeral to the memory of the person. For example, what was special about this person? What can be celebrated? What lessons can you learn from his or her life? If you have difficulty finding anything to work with here, you may choose to do an occasion- or gospel-oriented funeral service rather than a life-oriented one. (See Possible Funeral Formats.) Under no circumstances should you make up things about persons, thereby raising them to sainthood, or scandalize memory of them by focusing on their "dirty laundry." (See Respectful Remembrance of the Dead.) In addition, if any information that may be considered private is to be used in the service, such as cause of death, it should first be cleared with the family. (See Death by Suicide.)

When possible, tailor funerals to the deceased. To your joy, you will discover that not much extra time is needed to make the service reflect the person. (See the tribute section for some ideas.) Ministering with that little extra will enhance the kingdom and make you feel better about yourself and your calling.

Meaningful versus "For Show" Funeral

Sometimes you may be tempted to spend time on a funeral in direct relation to how many people will attend. However, if you find yourself going the extra mile only because there will be a huge crowd there, you are standing on the ethical line verging on vanity. Perhaps here an honest question would be, "Will I provide a meaningful service for the homeless individual as well as for the prominent community member?" God loves them equally. The challenge here is to be true "to God and the Scriptures," as well as "to yourself and your calling."

On the other hand, preparing for funerals and spending time with the grieving may easily become all consuming. While grieving people are to receive priority, you still need to have that Sunday sermon ready and minister to the rest of your congregation. Thus, after you have made sufficient effort, you need to deem the funeral service preparation adequate. It does not necessarily need to be exceptional, nor will it ever be perfect. Seek a healthy balance between striving for excellence and deeming your work adequate given your time frame.

Stealing Grief

Unfortunately, many pastors are uncomfortable with tears and have a great need to "fix it" when someone breaks down and weeps. At funerals and during the extended time of grief, giving in to this inner urge can be detrimental to the family of the deceased. Christ commanded us to mourn with those who mourn, and then he showed us how when he wept at Lazarus's tomb. Can you do the same and allow the grieving to experience the healing of tears? Or will you try to take away the survivors' grief by making them feel guilty for feeling pain? Glib comments such as "Give it all to Jesus"; "They are in a much better place"; "God works all things together for good"; "We don't have to mourn"; and "We should rejoice" often hurt more than they help. Allow people to grieve. Give them time to work through the intense pain of loss. It takes the average person one to three years to do this. Beware of stealing grief from those who need its healing power, and seek "to be true to God and the Scriptures" and "to the individuals involved." A helpful resource that further develops this theme is Doug Manning's *Don't Take My Grief Away*.[1]

Family Secrets
People carry interesting things to their death beds. Sometimes some of these things come out just prior to, or during, the funeral arrangements. For example, perhaps the individual was estranged from his or her spouse and living with someone else. How is the "live-in" to be mentioned in the obituary, and where will this person be seated at the funeral? These arrangements need to be negotiated with the family.

Or perhaps a child was born out of wedlock, given up for adoption, and kept a secret. Is this child mentioned at the funeral? Again, the family's wishes must be honored. When the family members have differing views, seek to negotiate a mutually acceptable response, in the privacy of an office, when counseling the family or planning the funeral.

Another example of secrecy may be the cause of death. What does the family wish to be made clear, and what should remain private? This is especially important around suicide (see below for special instructions on this funeral) and debilitating illnesses like AIDS or alcoholism. Even though you may rightly assume that some of this information is common knowledge, you should be sensitive to the family and discuss with them what is appropriate to focus on, or mention, in the funeral service.

Being "true to God and the Scriptures" as well as "to the individuals involved" are the challenging ethical issues in this case. It is not advisable to use someone as the ultimate example of the consequences of sin, even though this may appear to be "true to God and the Scriptures." Seeking to be true to the family will help temper this desire, or when the family desires such a service, "being true to yourself and your calling" will help you avoid such "good intentioned" fire-and-brimstone revenge. Speaking more generically of life choices and consequences would be more helpful.

Choosing a Casket

While some states and provinces regulate how much influence salespersons can exert during the selection of a coffin (some require that the agent be out of the room when the choice is made), you may be asked to be involved in the process. Walking the grieving family through this stressful experience of choosing the last resting place is a meaningful ministry, but be careful in giving advice. Help the family make a good choice. This may mean helping them feel that it is okay to buy the less expensive casket, which they can afford, rather than the most expensive one. When people feel guilty in their grief, they tend to compensate by choosing more than they can afford. Helping families make a good choice may be tricky, as you don't want them to accuse you later of having talked them into being "too cheap." The key is to help them choose rather than talking them into anything. Here you must seek "to be true to yourself and your calling," as well as "true to the individuals."

Jewelry on the Body

Jewelry on the body is another interesting issue. Many families desire that the deceased wear favorite jewelry for the viewing. But what happens to that jewelry at the conclusion of the viewing? Is it removed or left on the body? This should be discussed with the family prior to the funeral and specific instructions given to the funeral director. (Most funeral directors will ask the family's preference.) I recommend encouraging the family to instruct the funeral director to remove jewelry after the viewing and to return it to them. Though some may feel it should stay with the deceased, hindsight may reveal a wish that they had saved a wedding ring or other item for a child or grandchild. You can serve as a helpful, neutral guide in helping the family make a sound decision here.

Memorial Gifts

Another area in which the pastor can give guidance is memorial gifts. An ethical issue arises when hundreds of dollars are spent on flowers or on memorial gifts to a worthy cause when the deceased's spouse does not even have enough funds to pay for the funeral expenses. Here you need to be sensitive to actual needs and help steer well-wishers in the most helpful direction. After all, the giving of memorial money was originally started as a practice to pay for funeral expenses. Though it is nice to give toward some lasting memorial, we need to be practical as well. An appropriate balance can be found so that the funeral is lovely with flowers and expenses are met. Here you must work toward being true to the surviving family and exercising good stewardship (being "true to the Scriptures").

Pastoral Reimbursement

Whether you will receive payment for your services is always an issue. Should you charge for doing a funeral? If so, how much? If not, is doing funerals just part of your normal ministry to people? Do different rules apply if the deceased was not a member of your church?

Fortunately, help is available. In most cases, the funeral home handles the accounting arrangements and, in their costs to the family, charges a "going rate" ministerial fee to the family. The funeral home then pays the pastor directly. This practice usually saves you from having to raise the issue.

While some families may choose to provide a monetary gift to the minister in addition to this fee, it would be unethical to solicit such a "double billing." Personal integrity and "being true to the individuals involved" are the relevant ethical guidelines.

Receiving Gifts

Part of grief and loss involves disposing of the deceased's belongings. Often family members offer things to the pastor. While the minister may choose freely to accept or refuse the gifts, it is unethical to use this vulnerable moment to ask for a family heirloom from the aged deceased's spouse when the rest of the family is not around. Be very careful about receiving, or influencing to receive, gifts, especially during intense grieving. Being "true to God, yourself, and your calling" is at stake here.

Weaning Personal Pastoral Care

Responding to grieving persons as soon as you hear of a death is essential, as is spending time with the family while making the funeral arrangements and during the viewing(s) and immediately after the funeral. A time will come, however, when you must involve others in the pastoral care network so that you can wean yourself from the still needy survivors and press on with the rest of your ministry. It is very important to replace yourself as a pastoral care giver with others of like mind while you phase out your personal attention. This weaning process will help avoid any unhealthy clinging that may occur. Personal integrity "to God, yourself, and your call" is the concern here. Do not remain the only care giver to the point where vulnerability and ego lead to an unhealthy relationship, or even an affair.

Personal integrity on the part of the minister is the recurring key throughout the above examples. The ongoing challenge is, given the intense emotions involved in the context of death, how to establish a positive and affirming answer to all four of our ethical question guidelines, especially when they sometimes appear to conflict.

- How can I be true to God and the Scriptures?
- How can I be true to myself and my calling?
- How can I be true to the church I am serving?
- How can I be true to the individuals involved?

Note
1. *Doug Manning,* Don't Take My Grief Away: What to Do When You Lose a Loved One *(San Francisco: Harper & Row, 1984).*

Pastoral Preparation for a Funeral

THE PHONE RINGS. The caller is anxious and distressed. She has just been informed of the death of a loved one and is reaching out for help from her pastor—you! How will you respond? What will you do for her? Where do you begin? The following material is arranged according to the typical sequence of events that occur when a pastor is first called upon to comfort the grieving and conduct a funeral.

Providing Pastoral Care

The process of death may be lengthy or instantaneous, depending on the circumstances. Here are some practical suggestions for dealing with the dying process.

Respond to the Death (or Dying) Immediately

It is a matter of ministerial ethics that you respond immediately to those in grief. Whether the death was sudden or long-expected, it comes with such finality that ministering to the grieving receives precedence over all other pastoral work and usually even over personal family commitments. The only exception to the latter may be if you are away on vacation with your family. A plan should be worked out with the deacon board and be set in place ahead of time to deal with this situation should it occur. The specific circumstances of the case will determine whether you should cut short your vacation to return for the funeral.

Responses to death vary extensively. Generally, the more sudden and unexpected the death, the more the pastor is needed immediately. However, the heartbroken loved ones, having viewed the slow demise of their family member, should never be ignored. In all cases, instant pastoral care is to be offered or simply given.

You may struggle with what to say, but it is more important to be there with the grieving than to have a treatise prepared. Caring presence is what is needed, and perhaps even a shoulder to cry on. Be a pastor first. The theologian may be needed more later.

Enter the Deathwatch

You may face a dilemma in situations where the death process has been prolonged. People suffering prolonged illnesses especially tend to have times of near death followed by brief periods of remission. How often should you respond to the deathwatch? How long are you to remain at the bedside of the dying each time?

Two indicators are helpful when making this decision. One is the need of the family. How are they coping with the deathwatch? Do they need support, or are they finding enough strength in one another? If they are doing reasonably well, simply checking in with them regularly is sufficient, daily in the early stages and every few hours or hourly closer to the end.

The second extremely helpful indicator is input from the

hospital staff. Build rapport with them, stay tuned to how they view the patient's condition, and have them call you when it is timely. Between the staff and family calling you as needed, the chances of your being there at the appropriate time is very high.

Help the Survivors Say Good-bye

The doctors and staff could not understand how the patient could continue clinging to a thread of life. Though there was absolutely no hope for recovery, something was still holding him among the living. Something was unresolved. Finally, in one of those rare spiritual moments, the man's wife leaned over and said, "I love you, dear. You can let go now. I'll be all right. Good-bye." A few moments later the patient relaxed, gave a big sigh, and passed away.

Such powerful moments cannot be programmed, but they do happen. Sometimes it is the need of the patient. Other times it is the need of family members. In either case, saying good-bye is a powerful time of closure. Many people regret never having the opportunity to say those final words. Many deaths never permit the opportunity. But at a deathwatch there is much opportunity. The pastor, as a sensitive catalyst, may be privileged to help the loved ones in this final farewell by talking to them, preferably in the privacy of a waiting room, and then being there with them and the patient to give them the support to say good-bye. You may even tell the patient the family would like to say their good-byes. Such times are holy moments. Linger in them as long as needed.

Be Present during the First Visitation with the Body

Ideally there was time for a final good-bye while the individual was still at least semiconscious. If not, then this initial visit after death becomes a graphic reality check for the survivors. The loved one really is dead, and we must say our final farewell. (If there is an open casket at the funeral, there will be one or more opportunities for this final farewell.)

In most cases, seeing the deceased's body for the first time is a very traumatic time for the surviving loved ones. If the scene occurs in the hospital, cooperate with the hospital staff in the preparation for this time. In most cases, the hospital staff needs a few private moments with the body to remove all the tubes or other life-sustaining apparatus. Helping the family leave the intensive care room for a few moments and then calling them back when the nurse indicates it is appropriate is a very practical ministry. Inviting a hospital chaplain to help in this process is also very appropriate, particularly if you are feeling overwhelmed.

If the first viewing occurs in the funeral home, you are wise to work as a team player with the funeral home director. He or she is experienced in these matters and usually takes the lead in bringing the family to their deceased loved one. This allows you to be in a supportive role, perhaps with those who need it most.

Once the viewing is complete, lead in a pastoral prayer, thanking God for the life that was lived and asking strength for the family in the time ahead. When the viewing is in the funeral home rather than the hospital, more time is available and you may invite the family to be seated for a time of sharing memories and appropriate Scriptures in addition to the time of prayer. These are special moments; do not rush through them.

Facilitate the Prayer Service, Wake, or Prayer Vigil

Different traditions surround the death experience. Perhaps the most common is for the family to gather at the funeral home the evening before the funeral for a family viewing. Sometimes this time is used to share memories, to read Scriptures and pray, or to invite family members to pray as they desire.

Other times the prayer service or vigil is very brief and happens just before the funeral. The family gathers in an appropriate room away from the public, has a time of prayer, and then is ushered in to the sanctuary for the funeral.

Another common alternative is for the viewing to be open to the public the whole day before the funeral, with the family being present at specified hours so that the community can offer them condolences and comfort.

Occasionally the tradition of a night vigil is used. In this case the family simply spends time with the deceased, praying, singing, quietly talking among themselves, perhaps even spending the entire night doing this prior to the funeral. This tradition is more common among Native Americans. While family members most often host these events, be available to facilitate individual aspects, as requested.

Purposes of the Funeral Service

Facing death is seldom easy. Death brings about so many emotions, so many unspoken final words, so much pain, such finality. While pastoral care in the face of death is challenging, so too is planning the funeral. Where are you to begin in adequately planning an appropriate funeral service? One helpful place to begin is to remember what you are trying to accomplish in a funeral. Try to achieve the following five purposes in each service.

Making It Safe for People to Grieve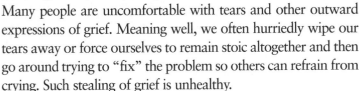
Many people are uncomfortable with tears and other outward expressions of grief. Meaning well, we often hurriedly wipe our tears away or force ourselves to remain stoic altogether and then go around trying to "fix" the problem so others can refrain from crying. Such stealing of grief is unhealthy.

God gave us tears because they help bring healing. Tears are very appropriate and should be affirmed at funerals. Weeping is a natural part of grieving the loss of a loved one, that special friend, sister, brother, mother, father, grandmother, grandfather, or other special person. Grieving people need love, comfort, consolation, and encouragement. But they especially need for it to be safe for them to cry. Christ calls us to mourn with those who mourn. Take time to do that at funerals, rather than working extra hard on trying to make the pain go away.

Respectfully Remembering the Deceased

What light in the deceased's life can be held up and honored? What from his or her life can be appreciated? Celebrate these events. Some people live a life that gives the pastor much material from which to work. Others make this task more challenging. The ethical issue here concerns honesty. You must not falsely fabricate stories or conversion experiences that never happened or are very questionable. Our purpose is not to build a saint in twenty minutes, but rather to truthfully remember the person, "warts and all." In a "good" funeral there should be laughter and tears as loved ones realistically remember the one now departed. Memories are very precious. How sad to sit through an entire funeral that is so generic the deceased is never even mentioned except by name in the eulogy.

Respectful remembrance is important even when the deceased does not deserve it. Even a scoundrel is a soul God loved and for whom Christ died. That person is someone's son, daughter, husband, wife, father, mother, or significant other. For those attending the funeral, there still is a loss, even if the loss is only of dreams of what might have been.

Though there may be little to work with, given a particular individual's life choices, the gift of life was given and now taken. As you stand in the holy presence of the Gift Giver, there is still room for respect. With dignity bid a final farewell to the earthly remains of that life.

Ministering to the Living

While the primary intent of the funeral is to respectfully remember the deceased, the key underlying focus is to minister to those who still remain. Since the deceased can no longer hear all that is being said, since he or she is no longer in pain or grief, you must minister to those who are. In other words, funerals respectfully remember the dead, but they also help the survivors begin to deal with their loss, unspoken feelings, pain and anguish, and to begin to rebuild their lives, which now will never "go back to normal." You must seek to put them on the path to building a new normality. How can you as pastor encourage them? How can you as God's servant extend God's comfort and love? How can you instill a glimmer of hope in an otherwise hopeless situation? How can you help the bereaved begin to desire to go on living? Certainly you cannot do all these things in a brief funeral service, but to instill even a ray of hope to the living is perhaps your most crucial task.

Showing Respect for the Gospel and Its Truth

How sad when, after consistently preaching that accepting Christ is the only way to the Father, pastors begin to waffle at a funeral and preach someone to heaven whom God simply cannot accept because of the choices made or, more importantly, the choice not made. You must be true to God and his Word and avoid raising the deceased to heaven or condemning him or her to hell when no one but God knows which direction the person went. A simple presentation of the gospel is still appropriate in these circumstances, but the application should be drawn to the living, not the deceased.

Helping People Face the Reality of Death and the Hope of Resurrection

The pastor's job is not to help people avoid the harsh finality of death, but rather to embrace it. Death is the logical outworking of life on this earth. Everyone, rich or poor, will one day pass through this same gate. That is reality, and a reality for which you must help people prepare.

The great hope that Christians hold of resurrection and life beyond the grave helps us best prepare for this final graduation to a whole new life. Help people see that death, even in its finality, is not the total end of all things, but rather a whole new beginning. But be careful when presenting this hope not to move to it so quickly that you steal people's grief away. (See Stealing Grief above.)

Focuses for the Funeral Service

When it comes to planning a funeral service, first choose what will be the major focus or orientation. Orientation is different than purpose, in that you generally choose only one orientation, whereas you seek to fulfill as many of the five purposes of the funeral as possible. There are essentially three orientations from which to choose.

Life-Oriented

Focusing on the deceased person's life can be the most difficult, and the most rewarding, service. A life-oriented funeral service is difficult because it must be original. Few things from previous funerals can be used, though principles remain consistent. You must research the person's life to draw out the content for your message. The time you spend visiting the family will provide essential material that you can skillfully weave into the fabric of the service. In addition to being a good listener, be sensitive to what the family would like aired and what they would prefer to be kept within family ranks only.

One helpful way to draw information is to ask family members to share some of their remembrances of the deceased. This works particularly well during the family viewing time or in the home where the family has gathered shortly after the death. Ask them what memories they would like to share and invite them to do so.

Another way to explore the deceased's life is to invite family members to compose a story or tribute about the person's life. Family groups, such as grandchildren, or all nieces and nephews, for example, do well at this task, bringing out laughter and tears in their honesty. It is especially moving if one of the writers can also read the story at the funeral.

Decorations, appropriate pictures of the deceased, significant items (such as a favorite baseball cap) displayed on the coffin, and favorite music all contribute to celebrating the life of the deceased. The family can do much to make this celebration appropriate and effective. While a life-oriented service takes effort, it is also the most rewarding to the pastor and to the family as a fitting remembrance to the loved one now departed.

Occasion-Oriented

From time to time funerals occur on or around a particular holiday. Depending on the significance of the day, the correlation may be better incorporated than ignored. For example, a funeral around Easter identifies more with the suffering of Good Friday—God understands losing a beloved child—than with the new life of Easter, yet the hope of new life is crucial to any funeral story. Use these seasonal themes.

Also falling in the category of occasion-oriented, though trickier, is cause of death. For example, if a young person has committed suicide, it is not unusual for friends, classmates, and even family members to be feeling comparable self-destructive emotions of despair. If the family of the deceased approves the idea, speaking about hopelessness and the need for seeking help may save someone else's life. Weaving this theme needs to be done extremely carefully, possibly even in consultation with a suicide prevention expert.

Sudden death by other means, such as vehicle accident, may also be used as a powerful reminder that death is ever near to each of us. Young age or vigorous health does not make a person immune to death. Sometimes funerals can be used to help the survivors take stock of what they are doing with their lives.

The occasion of death itself also is a great opportunity to speak about purpose in this life. Why are we here on this earth? Is death really the final end? Death forces each of us to struggle with our mortality and what we hold dear. What a great time to introduce God's love and purpose for us as human beings. Life is not meaningless. Rather, we are preparing in this life to live a far greater life beyond the grave with God. Living for him begins now. What a great purpose and meaning this brings to life on this sin-ridden earth.

Scripture-Oriented

Sometimes the circumstances of a death, or the life chosen by the deceased, does not lend itself to a life- or occasion-oriented service. A third option is choosing themes from Scripture.

One theme is a simple salvation message, particularly if many non-Christians are present. They need to hear that God loves them, sent his Son to die for them, and desires that they become his children. Keep the message simple and the attitude of love strong.

Another theme is comfort—how God comforts us in our affliction. Still another is the Good Shepherd who cares for us and binds up our wounds.

What was the deceased's favorite Scripture passage? This can also become the focus and be very effectively preached.

Scripture-oriented services can be a very practical choice, particularly when you have several funerals close together or a small community is impacted by several deaths and people need help in building a sound theology of death. Watch for the teachable moment and use it, but be careful not to forget the five purposes of the funeral. Minister to the grieving family and appropriately bury the deceased loved one.

Funeral Helps Based on Spiritual Commitment

Though each funeral is unique and should be treated accordingly, many fit into one of the following categories. Additional principles for funeral preparation can be drawn from these suggestions and applied to the specific situation at hand.

The Committed Christian

As much as a funeral can be, this type of funeral really is a worshipful celebration. Here lies a faithful child of God who remained faithful to the end and now has graduated to the life of which he or she often dreamed, a life in God's very presence. What a great opportunity to preach the reward of righteousness, the worthiness of remaining faithful, the value of choosing to live for God in this life and in the life beyond.

In addition to these great theological themes, burying a committed Christian is a wonderful opportunity for a life-oriented service celebrating God's faithfulness in the person's life throughout the years. As much as possible, involve family members in telling their stories of what the deceased meant to them and how their lives were impacted.

The Nominal Christian

This funeral is more difficult than the "committed Christian" funeral, because there were fewer clear instances of faith expressed that can be celebrated. In this case, focus on one or two noteworthy qualities or aspects of the person's life rather than trying to encompass his or her entire lifestyle. Thus an event- or occasion-focused service, or a gospel-focused service, is perhaps better than a life-oriented service. Try to avoid making a judgment on the person's spiritual quality of life.

Uncertain Spiritual Commitment

"Avoid condemning to hell or preaching them to heaven" is the best advice for this type of funeral. God is the judge, not any of us. Allow God to make that decision. Assurance of salvation still could be the focus of this service, for you can preach confidently that if we do turn to God, God will turn to us. Funerals cause those in attendance to consider their own mortality and therefore provide a wonderful opportunity for them to make their own salvation sure. While it is too late for the deceased to change, the funeral sermon may be timely for the living. Focus on their need with caring and gentleness.

The Agnostic

As he was dying, he writhed in agony and fear. He had rejected God out of bitterness, and now he was facing eternity without Christ. His death process was far from peaceful, dramatizing to me the great difference between dying with Christ or without Christ. Interestingly, I didn't need to be concerned about performing this funeral. There wasn't one. The unbelieving family simply chose to dispose of the body. No funeral. No memorial service. No reminder that this person had ever lived. How sad and terribly hopeless.

Should family members of an open agnostic choose to have at least a funeral, or even only an interment service, the minister is called upon to provide a ray of hope. Though opportunity for the deceased is past (though perhaps in the final moments he or she did make a commitment, like the thief on the cross), opportunity for the living to hear the simple gospel of God's great love is very present. Represented at the service may well be people who will never darken the door of a church. Preach God's love to them. They probably already know about hell and judgment.

The Atheist
It is remarkable that a church funeral would even be chosen in memorial of an atheist. God's love must have broken through to some family member. Preach to the living, explaining God's love and gently encouraging them to respond to it. Don't focus on the spiritual choices of the deceased. Instead, recognize and respectfully remember the life that was lived.

Additional Ideas for Delicate Funerals

One of the major challenges of pastoral life is performing funerals in especially sensitive situations. Since their emotions are already stretched, it is very easy to offend the grieving. Thus you must take special care when preparing a funeral that is complicated by delicate issues. Examples with guidelines on how to carefully handle each situation follow.

Death of a Young Mother or Father
People are especially touched when a young parent dies and small children are left without one or both parents. The two most common questions asked, one theological and the other practical, are: "How could a loving God allow this to happen?" and "Should the children be allowed to view the deceased parent?" Both questions deserve a response.

"How could God . . ." has been asked by countless individuals in numerous challenging situations or traumatic incidents. It arises from the more fair minded. Harsher persons blame God as the ultimate cause of the disaster: "How could God take my loved one!" or "A loving God would never take my loved one!" While the funeral is not the place to give a theological apologetic on justifying God's action, it is the place to gently nudge people in the direction of God's open and comforting arms. Though they are angry with God, God still loves them. Encourage people to honestly bare their feelings before God, to talk through their pain with someone who cares, to reassess their now fragile faith. Most of all they need to hear that God does still care, even though they perhaps are not yet ready to hear this important truth. Plant the seed and then nurture it throughout the lengthy grieving process that follows the funeral.

At the funeral of a young parent, remember especially the children left behind. Talk to them. Hug them if they will allow you to do so. Try to answer their blunt questions truthfully, avoiding phrases like "Mommy [or Daddy] has gone away to be with Jesus." To a child, going away implies the lost parent will return, as he or she has from every other trip. More appropriate is to speak about the pet that died and never came back or allow them to say what death is. Whether in pastoral care or in the funeral itself, graciously help children and adults wrestle with the reality, and finality, of death.

As to the question of a child viewing the deceased, allow the child to choose as he or she is able. Forcing children to view the body is unhealthy, but if they express a desire to do so, accompany them as they approach the casket. Seeing the deceased, in the company of a sensitive and caring adult, can provide helpful closure to the grieving child.

Death of a Child

Someone once said that to bury a parent is to bury the past, to bury a peer is to bury the present, but to bury a child is to bury the future. This is what makes a child's funeral so difficult. All the hopes and dreams for the child are lost in a moment of time, and the grief is extremely heavy.

There are no easy answers here as to "why," nor should we try to give any. Death is no respecter of age. We are left to cling to the Almighty, the only strength that can carry us through, or turn our backs on God and lose the only source of our ultimate future. The stakes run very high. Thus pastoral care needs to be sensitive and longsuffering.

In this funeral, recognize the life that was, the brevity lived, the unfulfilled dreams left behind. Rather than trying to answer ultimate questions, offer God's support and presence for the days ahead. Share the pain, even with tears, and plant the seed of hope that although life right now is shattered, God will walk with us through our pain, anger, and bewilderment. Try not to go forward too quickly.

Death of a Newborn/Stillborn

For months the young couple had been preparing the nursery, painting a mural on the wall, setting up the necessary furniture, buying baby supplies—arranging everything just right for their little bundle of life that was to come. But in place of the ecstatic joy was incredible grief as the couple stared at the tiny, lifeless form in the small casket. How could this have happened? Was this all just an incredibly awful nightmare? Unfortunately, it was real, and the couple would have to return to that empty house with the special room that would now remain empty.

Those closest to the infant will feel the pain the most. Though no one else may even have seen the child, the memories of that child and what may have been are very real. It is heartless to respond to the grieving with, "Well, you can always have other children." Our society, and even the Christian community, tends to downplay or overlook altogether the grief in this situation and the need for closure that a funeral gives. Work with the family to make this funeral meaningful. Focus on the grief and loss of dreams. Share the pain. Since this funeral cannot build on a life lived, it begins with the life lost and focuses on the needs of those remaining.

Another possible theme is scriptural. Draw on passages that show that God does still care, that God is not punishing the parents for their sins by taking the life of the child. Alleviating guilt would be a wonderful benefit of such a funeral.

Death of an Unborn Baby (Miscarriage)

Although a death certificate and burial are required by law for a stillborn (usually any child that reached the age of six months in the womb), miscarriages are often treated "as something you just have to get over." Even though the baby's life was not yet fully developed, the immediate family still experiences a real loss. Counsel the family to recognize this loss with a funeral if there is a body or, if not, at least with a memorial service. Encourage the couple and other family members to use this significant time of grief to help bring closure to their lost dream.

One practical idea in the memorial service is to use a lit candle, representing the lost life, as a focal point. A sense of closure for one father came after the service when he extinguished the candle.

Often the miscarriage is kept secret. If this is a couples' choice, respect their privacy. However, this choice also means they must bear all the pain alone. How much healthier it is to have them share their pain, at least with family and close friends, at a brief memorial service.

Death by Suicide

This funeral is one of the most challenging, because the individual chose to end his or her own life. Several issues need to be considered when preparing this funeral.

Of essential importance are the wishes of the family regarding making public the cause of death. If the public is not aware of the suicide, some families will prefer to keep it that way, and you need to respect their privacy.

Other families will prefer that the pastor reflect on the suicide during the funeral address, gently bringing it to light or addressing what is already commonly known. Especially powerful here is to speak about the temptation to end one's life when things are rough. Encourage people to pursue alternatives instead, such as seeking help or talking with a trusted friend. Especially when there is danger of a suicide pact, someone attending the service might be on the verge of harming himself or herself. You need to try your best to talk them out of this decision. Having professional help readily available for these people and even, as minister, seeking professional help in how to address the issue at the funeral, are very appropriate. Careful exposure of the tragedy at hand can be a great beginning for the healing process.

A third issue is theological in nature. "How does God view a person who takes his or her own life?" is a question that will be on many people's minds. Does such an act warrant losing one's salvation? Some people feel it does. Is the act sinful? Most would think it is. Should this theological issue be dealt with at the funeral? The pastor needs the wisdom of Solomon to decide this one, given the individual situation. Again, the primary focus must be the five purposes of the funeral outlined earlier. Theological reflection comes only as a secondary theme, and only if there are a significant number of people wrestling with the issue. It probably is more appropriate to deal with the theological issue at a subsequent church service or Bible study.

If the suicide was effected through a self-inflicted wound, the condition of the body may raise the issue of whether to choose a closed casket service. *(See below.)*

A Violent Death

Two senior high students went on a shooting rampage at their school. When the fury ended, one teacher and fourteen students lay dead, including the two gunmen. What would you say at a funeral for one of the deceased or for one of the gunmen?

Human tragedy draws crowds. Thus violent-death funerals are widely attended by people from all walks of life and from a variety of faith backgrounds. The community comes seeking meaning and hope. What would you say at such a funeral?

Much prayer must go into preparation for such a funeral, so that your "moment in the spotlight" does not become the primary focus. Instead, focus on the life that was, before it was snuffed out. Deal with the pain and senselessness of such a death. Focus on the hope and strength that knowing God personally brings. Paint a picture of life beyond the grave. But be careful to avoid condemning the perpetrator to hell. Revenge is the Lord's, not ours. God will take care of that part.

Most of all, avoid easy answers. If ever there is a time to mourn with those who mourn, this is it. The pain will not go away easily or quickly. As a pastor in the community, you need to be there for the long haul, walking with the hurting. Build a bridge to this time for ministry during the funeral by letting love and caring show. Be a channel of God's unconditional love.

A Sudden or Accidental Death

"He had just retired five months ago and was found dead on his exercise bike." "She was just driving to the corner grocery store but never came back, the victim of a drunk driver." "It was a freak accident they said. It just happened so fast."

When sudden death strikes, there is no time to prepare. Death is simply thrust upon us without warning, and we are left numb and in great shock. Often this shock is peppered with feelings of disbelief (Did this really happen?) and/or anger (How could this have happened?). Perhaps the most often asked question in response to sudden death is "Why?" As pastor you must be careful not to answer this question too quickly, for there is no simple answer. We can never fully understand God's ways. During the heat of immediate grief when the grieving blame God for causing the death is not the time to defend God's actions. Seeking someone or something to blame is a normal human reaction. God has bigger shoulders than anyone else, and he can take the heat until the anger of the grieving can be processed over time. Give people space to grieve as they need to express it. Walk alongside. Being there may well be far more important than the actual words you speak.

Death after a Prolonged Illness

Although this type of death gives family members adequate time to prepare for the ending of a life, they still feel a solemn finality. Don't be too hasty in assuring family members that the individual "is better off" and "is now pain free." While these references are true and can bring some measure of comfort, they can abort the healing process of grief. A death has still occurred. The final hour has come. Allow the finality to be real and work from there based on the circumstances the deceased leaves behind. For example, the funeral for a young mother losing her fight against cancer will be significantly different than that for an elderly man suffering his final illness. Some of the comments made in earlier paragraphs of this section may be appropriate to the particular need of the moment.

A Double or Multiple Death

They had been married for sixty-three years. Their death by natural causes came three days apart. What a beautiful celebration it was to bury them side by side, partners in life, now partners in death.

This type of funeral should be a celebration of life together, for there is much to celebrate. You must be careful, however, not to paint too rosy a picture of dying together, for it might encourage survivors of deceased spouses to take their own lives when their loved ones die. Keeping your audience in mind as you prepare this funeral will help you find a good balance here.

Other more difficult scenarios also fit into this category of double or multiple deaths. Perhaps the most common causes are vehicle accidents or acts of violence. Reading the sections above about Accidental Death and Violent Death will be helpful.

Unique to a multiple funeral is that the pain of grief is even more intensified. Seek to channel that pain into appropriate outlets rather than into bitterness or plans for revenge. Love for the hurting is the greatest message. They may not be ready to hear anything else right now.

Another possible reaction to multiple deaths is survivor's guilt. "Why were they taken, and I was left?" is the question that permeates this very real feeling. Address this question gently if there is evidence that it is being asked. Treat it as real, for it is a painful reality. Minister to the living and, by doing so, perhaps help save their lives.

Death Necessitating a Closed-Casket Funeral

Suicide may result from a self-inflicted wound that badly mars the body. Accidents, especially where fire is involved, may leave a body unrecognizable. A body found several days (or weeks) after death has begun to decompose. These and other situations leave a viewing of the deceased a questionable option. In some cases, a closed-casket service is the only choice, while in other circumstances, regardless of the condition of the body, the family may simply prefer a closed casket. Work with the family in making this choice, and help them recognize the closure issues involved.

Grief tends to distort one's view of reality, and without loved ones actually seeing the deceased's body, it may be hard for them to believe that he or she is really gone. As a result, the finality of death takes much longer to accept emotionally. When the body is viewable, the pastor might encourage the family to have a private viewing at least to say their final good-bye. Many people need the support of a caring pastor for this extremely difficult step, so be prepared to be present with them for this viewing.

If the body cannot be reasonably restored to make a viewing advisable, in your conversations with the family, affirm the funeral director's advice not to view the remains. A gruesome final view may be more damaging than no final viewing at all. Should the authorities require identification of the body by a family member, accompany the chosen person and support him or her through this overwhelming task.

For a closed-casket funeral service, a framed recent photo of the deceased, placed on or near the casket, can be a helpful focal point and reminder of the lost loved one throughout the service.

Organizing the Funeral Service

The pastor was in the midst of sermon preparation when the phone rang. The distressed caller reported that a death had occurred. Could the pastor come? Dropping everything, the pastor rushed to be with the survivors. After the pastor provided initial pastoral care to the grieving, the discussion moved toward planning the funeral. The pastor would have benefited from carrying in his or her Bible a checklist, such as the one included in Appendix H, to assist in this planning. Such a planning sheet is a helpful tool for discussing funeral details with the deceased's family, and using it helps avoid missing something significant. Writing in the answers also aids the pastor in remembering specifics requested by the family.

Funeral Planning Checklist

This worksheet addresses the details of the time and location of the viewing, funeral service, and interment, and whether a funeral home will be involved. It invites the family to consider and make plans for a reception held after the funeral: Where will it be held? Who will provide and serve the food? Too, the checklist asks about the persons involved in the funeral service—the pallbearers, pianist or organist, soloist, ushers, eulogizer, etc.—and elements of worship to be included in the service, such as the favorite hymn or Scripture passage of the deceased. If the funeral home does not take responsibility for compiling information for the service bulletin, you might need to help the family think about these details, in addition to putting together a biographical sketch of the deceased. The checklist also raises the question of whether the family would prefer to establish a memorial in lieu of, or in addition to, flowers. Such financial gifts could be earmarked for a favorite charity, for the support of surviving family members, for a scholarship fund, or for research toward a cure for the disease that took the deceased loved one (e.g., the American Cancer Society, if the deceased died of cancer).

This simple checklist is a wonderful tool for arranging all the details that need to occur during a time when emotions and forgetfulness run very high. Having the form readily available at a moment's notice is also extremely helpful. Appendix H is a one-page version of the form that you may reproduce for your own use.

Working with the Funeral Director

Funeral homes vary greatly in the services they provide and in the way they provide their services. Learn to work well with the local funeral director(s) in an effort to provide the best funeral service possible. Take the initiative to meet the funeral director(s) shortly after moving to a new pastoral ministry to build teamwork and to become acquainted with how funerals are typically done in the community. Novice pastors may want to volunteer to do funerals at the funeral home as needed. This experience will greatly help them sharpen these unique ministry skills, ideally before they are needed for a funeral within the current church.

While funeral homes take care of most of the following arrangements, check the following details with the funeral home or the family of the deceased (see Appendix I).

- Has a grave plot been selected?
- Is a family plot desired?
- Which cemetery is being used?
- Has grave digging been arranged?
- Have arrangements been made for a headstone (if desired)?
- Has a casket been chosen?
- If cremation is chosen, will there be a viewing first? If yes, are there rental caskets available?
- What is to be done with the deceased's ashes?
- In the case of a memorial service, closed-casket funeral, or a cremation without a viewing, is there a framed, recent portrait of the deceased available for display during the funeral service?

- Is additional transportation of the body needed?
- Who is preparing the bulletin?
- Who is placing the announcements of the funeral on the radio and in the newspaper?

Legal Documentation

Although the funeral home will need the deceased's social security number (U.S.) or social insurance number (Canada), the death certificate is the only legal document involved in the death event. That document is signed by the attending physician. As a result, no special clergy credentials are needed to conduct a funeral. In Canada the funeral home gives a copy of the Burial Permit to the minister to be kept on file at the church.

Typical Elements in a Funeral Service

A funeral service usually includes some or all of the following elements: musical prelude, processional, opening remarks, invocation, hymn(s), Scripture reading(s), eulogy, tribute, prayer of thanksgiving for the life of the deceased, special music, the funeral address, benediction, musical postlude, and recessional. The committal (or interment) service is typically more simple, featuring only some Scripture readings, brief pastoral remarks, a prayer, and benediction. These elements should be adapted to fit the current need. A reproducible copy of a Funeral Service Elements Checklist is available in Appendix J.

Personalizing the Funeral Service

"Let's see. I have my three generic funeral services. Which one should I use for this situation? It might be fairly large, so I'd better use service number two."

Sound familiar? It is particularly tempting to follow this pattern when an unexpected death bursts into your already hectic schedule. There is nothing wrong with reworking an existing funeral service when preparation time is short. But the key is reworking. How will you fit a preplanned service to the particular deceased person in this funeral? How you personalize a funeral service makes the difference between a meaningful funeral and a generic, one-size-fits-all funeral.

To personalize a funeral service, begin thinking about the deceased and what was special about him or her. If you knew the person well and have a lot of good material to work with, you could choose a life-oriented service (see above) and truly celebrate the life that was lived and the choices made.

If, on the other hand, you know very little about the person who died, you will need to spend enough time with family members that you "get to know" the deceased and are able to let his or her life permeate the service. What stories are appropriate to relate? (Discuss this with the family.) What incidents or events in the person's life should be recognized? What were his or her favorite songs, Scriptures, wishes, and so on. A little bit of sleuthing goes a long way in personalizing a funeral service, and it is very much worth the extra effort.

When very little information is available on the deceased, you may choose an occasion-based or theme-based service. Still it is important to speak about the deceased by name, focusing on a real life that has ended, though the content of that life may remain mysterious to you.

Involving Family Members

Family members vary extensively in how they handle grief. For some the last thing they desire is to stand in front of the audience and speak about the deceased. They simply cannot handle such an activity, and you as minister need to respect the space they need.

Other family members desire to speak at the funeral, sharing some of their memories and paying their last respects. This is an important part of their grieving process. Much of this sharing is especially fitting at the family viewing times. Some of this sharing is very appropriate at the funeral. Perhaps even "opening up the mike" at the funeral service will allow people to share what is on their hearts. If planning to do this, however, tell the family ahead of time so they can be prepared to share if they desire. Also, mentioning this opportunity at the beginning of the funeral service and then providing it near the end gives the audience time to think of what they would like to share. If you choose to provide such an opportunity, be careful not to drag the opportunity out or force the unwilling to speak.

Between those unwilling to speak and those willing to speak are those who need your encouragement to share their grief and memories publicly. Helping them write out what they want to say, assuring them of your presence with them at the funeral, offering to finish reading the material for them if they break down, and assuring them that tears are just fine all greatly help family members be involved meaningfully in their loved one's funeral service. This involvement makes for a powerful, personalized service.

Including a Tribute

Particularly appropriate at a funeral is the writing and reading of a tribute to the deceased. Children and grandchildren are particularly good at this, for their honesty and forthrightness stir both laughter and tears, making the deceased's influence very real. The writing may be an individual or group effort, but each usually requires a sensitive pastor to plant the seed of the idea and to nurture the product that develops. When possible, a tribute is best read by its author.

Burial of the Body, the Final Farewell

"Spread my ashes over the Rocky Mountains" was the deceased's final request. Could the request be fulfilled, or should the family just ignore it and proceed as they choose? This is a decision the family needs to make, with sensitive encouragement and gentle support from the pastor. Help them do what they need to do. Try to be flexible.

In our society, survivors of the deceased have a choice as to what is done with a body. The variety of options include graveside burial, cremation, entombment, memorial service only, or family burial. Each option has choices within itself, with implications for the pastor's portion of the service.

Graveside Service

After the church or chapel funeral, most funerals conclude with a final brief ceremony at the cemetery. Depending on the circumstances, one or more of the following options may be used.

Public Graveside Service

In many cases, those who attend the funeral are invited to follow the hearse to the cemetery. There a canopy has been set up with some chairs provided by the funeral home for the immediate family. Most graveside services are very brief, usually with appropriate Scriptures, a few final words of comfort, and a committal prayer. It is a time of final farewell, and for some who grieve, this finality will be the most difficult moment.

The specific style of this service varies somewhat from region to region. In some areas the coffin is placed on the guide belts over the grave, the service is conducted, the people say their final farewell, a flower may be taken from the arrangement on the coffin and given to the immediate family members (or children and/or grandchildren place a flower on the coffin), and all leave before the coffin is lowered into the grave and sealed in its encasement.

In other regions, the group remains to watch the coffin being lowered into the ground. When I was growing up, the style was to lower the coffin into a wooden box. The wooden lid was then placed on the box and someone climbed in to nail it down securely. Then family members threw in the first few shovels of dirt, lending an immeasurable finality to the death. This practice is seldom followed today, although some areas are going back to this style.

Private Graveside Service

Some families choose to have a public funeral service but a private burial, allowing only family and perhaps a few select friends to be present. Styles here may also vary. Some families choose to have the burial service at a separate time from the funeral, either before or after the public funeral. This choice may be to accommodate family that must travel a great distance, or to let the family have a private final farewell. Appropriate at such a service is providing opportunity for family members to verbalize their good-byes, as they desire.

Military Rites at the Graveside Service

When the deceased is an armed services veteran, final military rites may be included at the graveside service. This option is provided by the local designated veterans organization. It involves having the casket draped with the country's flag, which is then ceremoniously removed at the graveside service, folded properly, and presented to the surviving spouse or family representative. A moment of silence follows, a trumpet farewell is played, or a twenty-one-gun salute is given (or all three may be chosen). Work with the family and the local Legion to decide what military rites will be observed.

Graveside Service during Inclement Weather
Since graveside services are at the mercy of the elements, some alterations may be required. While canopies help shield family members from wind, rain, or sun, extreme cold is harder to deal with effectively. While a heater under the canopy can help somewhat, in extreme conditions the public is invited to remain at the church for the return of family members. Then the family members follow the hearse to the graveside and, from their vehicles, view the placement of the coffin by the pallbearers. The funeral home then takes care of the rest of the details while the family returns to the church. When this format is necessary, elements of the committal service are simply added to the end of the funeral in the church service so that the final closure still occurs.

Entombment in a Mausoleum
Some communities offer the service of entombment in a mausoleum rather than burial in a ground plot. Essentially this means the casket is placed in a vault built into the cement walls of the mausoleum with an identifying plaque on the vault door. The mausoleum usually stands in a cemetery and, in addition to providing another alternative, becomes very practical as graveyards take up more and more of our land space. Services at an entombment are generally patterned after graveside services with the exception of comments such as, "We commit our loved one to the earth" or "We return them to the ground from which they came."

Cremation
Some families cannot stand the thought of their loved one's body undergoing decay. Others cannot afford the expense of a grave plot or are so mobile that choosing a location for a family plot is simply not feasible. Thus cremation of the body has become a popular option.

An interesting theological dilemma that may arise when the cremation choice is made, is that Christian people may be concerned about Christ's return and the faithful being reunited with their bodies. How can this happen if the body has been burned to ashes?

Give some thought to this issue, preferably before the question is asked. Some helpful ideas in response include the following. God is not limited when it comes to recreating matter. God has no second-class followers. Those whose bodies were destroyed in such ways as by war, fire, violent weather, or cremation will not be reduced to a lower level of eternity. Our resurrected bodies will be new anyway, with properties far greater than we have currently, and they will be similar to Christ's. Some may respond that Christ's resurrected body still bore recognizable scars (hands, feet, side), and this is true. We will not know a full final answer until we stand in the Lord's presence. But I don't believe cremation is an issue to worry about.

Memorial Service Only (No Body)

Sometimes circumstances dictate that no body is present at the funeral. This may occur when no body is found, when the body was destroyed, when immediate cremation was chosen, or for a host of other reasons. In some situations the body is present but the coffin was sealed prior to the funeral because of the body's poor condition, thus making viewing impossible.

The memorial service tends to flow very similarly to that of a regular funeral, with the exception that there is no physical focal point. The reality of death may be more evasive as a result, particularly in the case of sudden, unanticipated death. In light of these concerns, it is helpful to have a recent picture of the deceased or other artifact at the funeral to serve as a focal point and to aid with the reality of death.

Family Burial

A recent article in my local newspaper, The Forum, caught my eye. The essence of this article was that some families are choosing to take back the burial process. Largely because of expenses, but partially because of sentiment, families may legally choose to skip embalming, prepare the body themselves, dig the grave, and lay their loved one to rest. According to the article, the only legal necessities are a "burial-transit" or "disposition" permit for transporting the body to the gravesite and a death certificate from the doctor pronouncing the individual dead.

A minister, if invited to be involved, is compelled to be aware of regional legal requirements and to make sure of their fulfillment before proceeding with the funeral. The article did mention that six states—Connecticut, New York, Indiana, Nebraska, Louisiana, and New Hampshire—require the participation of a licensed funeral director in the burial proceedings.

{ 6 }
Funeral Service Resources

THIS CHAPTER CONTAINS examples of elements that can be adapted for use in funeral services. Pick and choose, creating your own unique service for each situation. You may download this chapter for your personal use from the Judson Press website (see Preface, XVII). Also, since each funeral element may be printed in a separate section, you can easily intersperse materials from your own funeral file.

Opening Remarks

How one begins a funeral service tends to set the tone for the entire experience. People in attendance are often nervous with the setting and the probable presence of a body. Some people are emotional, grieving their loss. Others are stony and trying to remain at arm's length. All present need warm and comforting words from a pastor to set them at ease. Add to or adapt the following material to fit the uniqueness of the deceased person and those family members and friends who grieve the loss of this loved one.

———⟨∾∾∾⟩———

Expected Death

Welcome to this sanctuary this afternoon as we gather to celebrate the long and full life of _____ (full name). In God's goodness, God granted her/him almost ___ years of life, so we have much to remember and to celebrate.

But amid our celebration of her/his life, we have also gathered to say our final farewell to _____ (first name), this mother/father and grandmother/grandfather (Oma/Opa as she/he was affectionately called by some). Saying good-bye to loved ones is never easy, and the finality of this type of good-bye is hardest of all. The pain of loss through death is very real. Tears, then, are appropriate at farewells.

Yet, while tears are an appropriate expression of our loss, the pain need not lead to despair and hopelessness among us who are left behind, for we are a people of faith and hope. We know that death is not the final end.

Amid our grief we recognize that _____'s pilgrimage on this earth is now over. She/he has begun a new life in a far better place, a place where she/he is no longer hindered by her/his physical limitations. May we find strength from this fact, freeing us to express both our tears and our joyful remembrances, as we share together in this special service. The Lord is also here to lovingly provide comfort and strength. Let us recognize God's presence through a prayer of invocation.

———⟨∾∾∾⟩———

Unexpected Death (Christian)

Welcome to this sanctuary this morning. We have gathered to both celebrate the life and grieve the sudden loss of

_____ (full name). Thus we come with mixed emotions, perhaps not exactly sure how to feel, because _____ (first name) was our dear daughter/son, or mother/father, or grandmother/grandfather, or great friend, and we loved our time with her/him so much, and now our relationship with her/him has ceased so unexpectedly.

But as we sit here grieving our loss, our minds cannot help but also be flooded with all the special memories we have of having spent time with this special person, _____ . Later in the service we will take just a few moments to allow you to share some of those memories if you would like to do so. Memories are so very precious, for they live on with us, though their source has now passed on.

And so we gather to share memories and to say a final farewell to _____ . During this service, we will laugh about some of the memories, perhaps like her/his driving, and we will cry about others, like the suddenness of her/his death, and both responses are very appropriate. A funeral is for grieving, for sharing our pain of finality and loss, for sharing some of those "if only I had done this" regrets. May we allow the tears to come and bring healing to our souls.

But a funeral such as this, of one who was ready to meet her/his Lord, is also a time of remembering and celebrating that life. May we touch one other with our inner joy as well as we share these precious moments and memories together.

God is also here to share our pain and our joy. Let us acknowledge the Lord's presence now through prayer.

———❧❧❧———

Accidental Death

Our hearts are heavy with grief as we gather together today to bid our final farewell to the young and precious life of

_____ (full name). Death has come suddenly and unexpectedly to painfully tear one of our loved ones from us. Yet, amid our pain, we desire to pay tribute to her/his short life, sharing the memories we have of _____ .

We remember _____ as the picture of health and vitality, as in her/his youthful exuberance, she/he tackled life on the run. We remember her/him as a friend, a _____ (sport) teammate, a much loved family member.

Thus, though death has tragically separated _____ from us, part of her/him will still live on with us forever; that part stored in the fond memories we have of time spent with her/him. These memories we will cherish and keep, a living testament of a daughter/son whose life span here on earth was so short.

It is out of love that we have gathered here today to mourn her/his passing, to lovingly pay to her/him our last respects, and to support one another in our grief. Looking down upon us in our sorrow is a Heavenly Father who also knows what it means to lose a child to death. It is the Lord who well understands what we all feel today, for God's only child died on this earth too. Let us turn to God's heart of love and compassion, even now, to welcome his comforting presence here and to invite him to come alongside us in our grief.

———*eɔɔ*———

Suicide

We have gathered as friends and family to pay tribute to the life and memory of _____ (full name).

We come with many mixed emotions. Many of us are still numb with shock, our minds reeling with the unnecessary waste of life that comes with a self-inflicted death. Others of us are struggling with feelings of remorse—"if only I had called," "if only I had been there," "if only I had been a closer friend," "if only I had picked up on the signs," "if only we could wish it all away."

Yet no matter what we wish, the reality remains. Death has invaded our lives with its usual coldness. But, then, death is never convenient or painless. It always bursts into our life as the grim, untimely reaper.

We are not alone, however. We are not a people without hope. God is here and still in control. Death is not the ultimate end for those of us who believe in God. Rather, it is the beginning of life in God's presence, a new and eternal life for which we have been created.

In mercy and grace, God has received _____ into his presence, as a believer who made a wrong choice. God is the giver and taker of life, not us. May we who remain always be careful to let God make that choice.

And so, in great sorrow, we gather to pay our last respects to the earthly remains of _____ , to remember her/his life and the fond memories of pleasant times with her/him.

We have also gathered to support and comfort one another in this time of deeply felt loss. If ever we needed one another, it is now.

And in our coming together, we also seek God's strength. We desire to lean on God's everlasting arms. May we all truly find strength for our souls in this time together.

—————

Death of Someone with Questionable Spiritual Commitment

As the minister of this church, and for many of you, your pastor and friend, I welcome you to this special service of remembrance today. We have gathered to pay tribute to the life and memory of _____ (full name).

Our presence here is indication that we knew _____ , either through a family, church, business, or community relationship, and we have come to mourn her/his passing and pay her/him tribute one last time.

In moments such as these, each of us finds our mind flooded with memories of our association with _____ . Our memories are varied, many good, some perhaps not so good, for no person is perfect, yet we are here to sort through those memories and choose the ones we will hold dear. It is these precious memories that we will always carry with us, long after today is past. Today is a day for choosing and sharing memories.

Today is also a day to reflect on the meaning and purpose of life here on this earth. Through facing a death, we all again realize that our bodies are not made to last forever. One day we too will pass into eternity. This thought is very sobering. But the good news is that Jesus has gone on ahead to prepare a place for us. Life here on earth is only preparation for the life to come. Yet we must choose in this life what will happen for us in the life to come. May we each respond to Christ's gracious invitation while there is time. He beseeches, "Come to Me, all who are weary and heavy-laden, and I will give you rest" (Matthew 11:28), and again, "I am the resurrection and the life; he who believes in Me shall live even if he dies, and everyone who lives and believes in Me shall never die" (John 11:25–26).

Let us bow in prayer and invite this great God who cares so much about each one of us to be present now and grant us strength and grace for this hour.

———*ᴓᴓᴓ*———

Death of Someone with No Spiritual Commitment

We have gathered today as a caring community to pay tribute to the life and memory of _____ (full name).

A funeral has a threefold purpose, the first of which is to grieve the loss of a loved one. As we think of _____, we immediately identify her/him as our friend, or sister/brother, or daughter/son, or mother/father, or grandmother/grandfather, or godmother/godfather. We have experienced a loving relationship with her/him, and that relationship has now been severed. The loss is ours, and it is painful. We have come to grieve that loss.

The second purpose of a funeral is to lovingly pay our last respects. It is only right that we make the time to come and bid the earthly remains of _____ a final farewell. By our presence we show our respect for her/him, admitting her/his place in life alongside us was significant and will be missed.

And, finally, a funeral provides a time for us to celebrate special memories of times spent with her/him. Funerals are an appropriate place to share some of those precious memories with one another.

And so, though we here confront the separation death brings, our minds cannot help but be flooded with blessed and joyful memories of times spent with _____ . Those precious memories will last forever in our hearts and minds, though we bury her/his body today. Her/his joyous spirit, kindness, thoughtfulness, her/his always being there to lend a hand, . . . are memories that will continue to influence us even with the passing of time. These vivid memories are a living testament of a person who sought to live life fairly and charitably in our community. Our lives are richer for having known _____ .

We come then, with mixed emotions. While the memories of her/his life are sweet, the pain of their passing is real. We find ourselves in need of a strength beyond our own. We find that strength in the arms of a loving and gracious God who is also present here with us. "God is our refuge and strength, a very present help in trouble" (Psalm 46:1, paraphrased).

The LORD is near to all who call upon Him,
To all who call upon Him in truth.
He will fulfill the desire of all who fear Him;
He will also hear their cry and will save them.
—Psalm 145:18–19

Let us turn even now in prayer to this God who hears.

Prayers of Invocation

To the God Who Provides Comfort and Strength

Thank you, gracious God, for your comforting presence here today. Thank you for wrapping your arms of unconditional love around us and filling us with your peace, even as we grieve the loss of our loved one, _____ . Thank you for the extra portion of comfort and strength you give for such a time as this. We worship you, O Lord, our strength. Amen.

To the Triune God Who Restores Life

Lord, in your Word you describe yourself as the resurrection and the life. You say that those who believe in you, though they die physically, will live eternally—they will never really die. Thus, though we stand here in the presence of physical death, we still have within us a living hope, a hope based on who you are.

Almighty God, you demonstrated your power over death when you raised up our Lord Jesus Christ from the grave. In these moments of memorial and mourning, we pray for your strengthening presence and a continued assurance of your power over death, the essence of our hope. Enable us, we pray, to worship you in openness and love, and through your Word to find patience and comfort for our present circumstance.

Through your power and strengthening presence, Holy Spirit, grant that our minds and hearts and faith may be raised above the shadows of mortality and brought into the light of your compassionate countenance and the security of your warm presence.

We pray this in the name of him who died and rose again and ever lives with us, Jesus Christ our Lord. Amen.

—————

To the Lord Who Gives Eternal Hope and Life

Lord of life, author of hope, victor over death, be present with us in these moments of memorial and grant to us the real experience of your living presence. In your infinite and unconditional love, be pleased to look down on our bereaved souls and enable us to hear your holy Word, that through the patience and comfort of the Scriptures, we may again find hope. Impart to our minds an understanding of life after death, to our hearts an assurance of that which we are invited to possess in Jesus Christ, and to our lives the courage to persevere in faithful living. By the power of Jesus Christ, who himself rose from the grave, comfort us and challenge us with the words of eternal life. Amen.

—————

To the God Who Strengthens

Father God, death has again struck with its awesome finality and taken one of our loved ones. We are hurting. We are struggling. We are wrestling to again find hope and meaning in life.

As we writhe in our pain, we are reminded that ultimate hope and meaning lie only in knowing you, in loving you, in seeking your will and way for our lives.

As death causes us, the survivors, to reassess our priorities, may we choose what is good and right. May we choose to make our peace with you, gracious Father, that we might have strength beyond our own to face this time of grief and cope with our life beyond the grave.

Loving God, please be our tower of strength both now and throughout our entire lives. We pray in the strong name of Jesus. Amen.

———— *ⁿⁿ* ————

To the God Who Is Present

Loving Father, thank you for your comforting presence and understanding as we have gathered here in our grief. We confess we are at a loss to understand why such a tragic accident had to happen, that has claimed the life of _____ . We are confused by such a sudden death. The only thing that we are still sure of, is that you love us. You are standing here with us in our pain. In fact, you are actually carrying us through this deep valley of the shadow of death.

Bear us up, Father, as we share the memories of this precious life that you gifted us with for such a short while. Strengthen us as the images we share touch anew our great sense of joy in a life shared and the hurt and loss of a life snatched from us. Grant that we might feel your great comfort and consolation in this needy hour. We need you, Lord. Sustain us and fill us with courage in this our time of raw and keen grief. Thank you for your caring presence here now. Thank you for the great difference knowing you makes, especially in the face of death, life's final enemy. Touch our hearts anew with your gracious love, even now. We pray in Jesus' name. Amen.

—◦◦◦◦—

To the God Who Forgives

Almighty God, maker of heaven and earth, we humbly bow in your presence this day, a people in deep sorrow and grief. We very much realize that life is a special and sacred gift from you and that to snuff out that life is a very serious thing. Yet we also know that you are a God of justice and mercy, a God who forgives sin even when the consequences of our actions bring irreversible results. Loving Father, assure us of your caring presence even now, and fill us with the hope that is ours in Christ, of life beyond the grave. Just as _____ loved you and had committed her/his life to you prior to this tragic event, we too reaffirm our commitment to you, that one day we too may stand with her/him in your nearer presence.

O God, you are indeed our refuge and strength, a very present help in time of trouble. Flood us with your warm comfort and grace that the keen sting of death we now feel may be lessened and that we may fittingly remember _____ in these moments of memorial. The _____ years of life which she/he did experience here on this earth were given by you, and we are thankful for them. And in the assurance of the life hereafter, which _____ also now enjoys, we find comfort and joy. Thus we can lift up our voices even in thanksgiving to you, for though we do not understand why, yet we would trust that you are still at work among us and will graciously lead us on from this moment of sorrowful tragedy.

To you, our source of forgiveness, strength, comfort, and direction, be glory forever and ever. Amen.

Appropriate Hymns

———❦❦❦———

Praise-Oriented

"Holy God, We Praise Thy Name"
"Praise to the Lord, the Almighty"
"Amazing Grace"
"Because He Lives"

———❦❦❦———

Comfort-Oriented

"Beyond the Sunset"
"God Will Take Care of You"
"In the Garden"
"Jesus Loves Me"
"Leaning on the Everlasting Arms"
"The Lord's My Shepherd"
"Near to the Heart of God"
"Rock of Ages"
"Under His Wings"
"Through It All"
"What a Friend We Have in Jesus"
"Safe in the Arms of Jesus"
"He Giveth More Strength"

———❦❦❦———

Response-Oriented (if appropriate)

"Just as I Am"
"Just a Closer Walk with Thee"

Relevant Funeral Scriptures

Traditional Texts of Hope

The LORD is my shepherd,
I shall not want.
He makes me lie down in green pastures;
He leads me beside quiet waters.
He restores my soul;
He guides me in the paths of righteousness
For His name's sake.

Even though I walk through the valley
    of the shadow of death,
I fear no evil; for Thou art with me;
Thy rod and Thy staff, they comfort me.
Thou dost prepare a table before me
    in the presence of my enemies;
Thou hast anointed my head with oil;
My cup overflows.
Surely goodness and lovingkindness will follow
    me all the days of my life,
And I will dwell in the house of the LORD forever.
—Psalm 23

God is our refuge and strength,
A very present help in trouble.
Therefore we will not fear, though the earth
    should change,
And though the mountains slip into the heart
    of the sea;
Though its waters roar and foam,

Though the mountains quake at its
      swelling pride....

"Cease striving and know that I am God;
I will be exalted among the nations,
      I will be exalted in the earth."
The Lord of hosts is with us;
The God of Jacob is our stronghold.
      —Psalm 46:1–3,10–11

———•———

There is an appointed time for everything. And there
      is a time for every event under heaven—
A time to give birth, and a time to die;
A time to plant, and a time to uproot
      what is planted....
A time to weep, and a time to laugh;
A time to mourn, and a time to dance....
A time to search, and a time to give up as lost;
A time to keep, and a time to throw away....
[God] has made everything appropriate in its time.
      —Ecclesiastes 3:1–2,4,6,11a

———•———

"Come unto Me, all who are weary and heavy-laden, and I will
give you rest."
      —Matthew 11:28

———•———

Jesus said . . . , "I am the resurrection and the life; those who
believe in me, even though they die, will live, and everyone who
lives and believes in me will never die."
      —John 11:25–26, NRSV

———•———

When Jesus finally got there, he found Lazarus already four
days dead. Bethany was near Jerusalem, only a couple of miles

145

away, and many of the Jews were visiting Martha and Mary, sympathizing with them over their brother. Martha heard Jesus was coming and went out to meet him. Mary remained in the house.

Martha said, "Master, if you'd been here, my brother wouldn't have died. Even now, I know that whatever you ask God he will give you."

Jesus said, "Your brother will be raised up."

Martha replied, "I know that he will be raised up in the resurrection at the end of time."

"You don't have to wait for the End. I am, right now, Resurrection and Life. The one who believes in me, even though he or she dies, will live. And everyone who lives believing in me does not ultimately die at all. Do you believe this?"

"Yes, Master. All along I have believed that you are the Messiah, the Son of God who comes into the world."

—John 11:17–27, THE MESSAGE

"Let not your heart be troubled; believe in God, believe also in Me. In My Father's house are many dwelling places; if it were not so, I would have told you; for I go to prepare a place for you. And if I go and prepare a place for you, I will come again, and receive you to Myself; that where I am, there you may be also. And you know the way where I am going." Thomas said to Him, "Lord, we do not know where You are going, how do we know the way?" Jesus said to him, "I am the way, and the truth, and the life; no one comes to the Father, but through Me."

—John 14:1–6

We do not live to ourselves, and we do not die to ourselves. If we live, we live to the Lord, and if we die, we die to the Lord; so then, whether we live or whether we die, we are the Lord's.

For to this end Christ died and lived again, so that he might be Lord of both the dead and the living.

—Romans 14:7–9, NRSV

For we know that if the earthly tent which is our house is torn down, we have a building from God, a house not made with hands, eternal in the heavens.

—2 Corinthians 5:1

And now, dear friends, we want you to be fully informed about the Christians who have "fallen asleep," so that you will not grieve as others do who have no hope. For since we believe that Jesus died and rose to life again, so also we believe that God will bring back with Jesus those who have "fallen asleep" in Him.

We tell you this on the Lord's authority: we who are alive and remain until the coming of the Lord will certainly not precede those who have died. For the Lord Himself will descend from heaven with a shout of command, with the archangel's call and with the sound of the trumpet call of God, and the dead in Christ will be the first to rise. Then we who are alive and remain will be caught up together with them in the clouds to meet the Lord in the air, and be forever with the Lord. So comfort one another with these thoughts.

—1 Thessalonians 4:13–18, *The New Translation*

Blessed be the God and Father of our Lord Jesus Christ, who according to His great mercy has caused us to be born again to a living hope through the resurrection of Jesus Christ from the dead, to obtain an inheritance which is imperishable and undefiled and will not fade away, reserved in heaven for you.

—1 Peter 1:3–4

Calling for God's Strength

My God, my God, why hast Thou forsaken me?
Far from my deliverance are the words of my groaning.
O my God, I cry by day, but Thou dost not answer;
And by night, but I have no rest.
Yet Thou art holy,
O Thou who art enthroned upon the praises of Israel.
In Thee our fathers trusted;
They trusted, and Thou didst deliver them.
To Thee they cried out, and were delivered;
In Thee they trusted, and were not disappointed. . . .

Yet Thou art He who didst bring me forth from
     the womb;
Thou didst make me trust when upon my
     mother's breasts.
Upon Thee I was cast from birth;
Thou hast been my God from my mother's womb.
               —Psalm 22:1–5,9–10

I waited patiently for the Lord;
And He inclined to me, and heard my cry.
He brought me up out of the pit of destruction,
     out of the miry clay;
And He set my feet upon a rock making my
     footsteps firm.
And He put a new song in my mouth,
     a song of praise to our God;
Many will see and fear,
And will trust in the Lord. . . .

Thou, O Lord, wilt not withhold Thy
      compassion from me;
Thy lovingkindness and Thy truth will
      continually preserve me.

—Psalm 40:1–3,11

God is our refuge and strength,
A very present help in trouble.
Therefore we will not fear,
      though the earth should change,
And though the mountains slip into the
      heart of the sea;
Though its waters roar and foam,
Though the mountains quake at its swelling pride....

"Cease striving and know that I am God;
I will be exalted among the nations,
      I will be exalted in the earth."
The Lord of hosts is with us;
The God of Jacob is our stronghold.

—Psalm 46:1–3,10–11

Why are you in despair, O my soul?
And why have you become disturbed within me?
Hope in God, for I shall again praise Him
For the help of His presence.
O my God, my soul is in despair within me;
Therefore I remember Thee from the land
      of the Jordan,
And the peaks of Hermon, from Mount Mizar.
Deep calls to deep at the sound of Thy waterfalls;
All Thy breakers and Thy waves
      have rolled over me.

The Lord will command His lovingkindness
in the daytime;
And His song will be with me in the night,
A prayer to the God of my life.

—Psalm 42:5–8

The Comfort We Receive from God

When you pass through the waters,
I will be with you;
And through the rivers, they will not overflow you.
When you walk through the fire,
you will not be scorched,
Nor will the flame burn you.
For I am the Lord your God, The Holy One of Israel,
your Savior.

—Isaiah 43:2–3a

I will comfort you there as a little one is comforted by its mother.

—Isaiah 66:13, TLB

And we know that all that happens to us is working for our good if we love God and are fitting into his plans.

—Romans 8:28, TLB

Who shall separate us from the love of Christ? Shall tribulation, or distress, or persecution, or famine, or nakedness, or peril, or sword? Just as it is written,

"For Thy sake we are being put to death all day long;
We were considered as sheep to be slaughtered."

But in all these things we overwhelmingly conquer through Him who loved us. For I am convinced that neither death, nor life, nor angels, nor principalities, nor things present, nor things to come, nor powers, nor height, nor depth, nor any other created thing, shall be able to separate us from the love of God, which is in Christ Jesus our Lord.

—Romans 8:35–39

The Strength and Peace We Have in Knowing God Personally

So now, since we have been made right in God's sight by faith in his promises, we can have real peace with him because of what Jesus Christ our Lord has done for us.

For because of our faith, he has brought us into this place of highest privilege where we now stand, and we confidently and joyfully look forward to actually becoming all that God has had in mind for us to be.

We can rejoice, too, when we run into problems and trials for we know that they are good for us—they help us learn to be patient. And patience develops strength of character in us and helps us trust God more each time we use it until finally our hope and faith are strong and steady.

Then, when that happens, we are able to hold our heads high no matter what happens and know that all is well, for we know how dearly God loves us, and we feel this warm love everywhere within us because God has given us the Holy Spirit to fill our hearts with his love.

—Romans 5:1–5, TLB

What a wonderful God we have—he is the Father of our Lord Jesus Christ, the source of every mercy, and the one who so wonderfully comforts and strengthens us in our hardships and trials. And why does he do this? So that when others are troubled, needing our sympathy and encouragement, we can pass on to them this same help and comfort God has given us.

You can be sure that the more we undergo sufferings for Christ, the more he will shower us with his comfort and encouragement. We are in deep trouble for bringing you God's comfort and salvation. But in our trouble God has comforted us—and this, too, to help you: to show you from our personal experience how God will tenderly comfort you when you undergo these same sufferings. He will give you the strength to endure.

—2 Corinthians 1:3–7, TLB

Scripture Medleys

Adding various related Scriptures together produces a powerful tool of encouragement and strength. Here are three examples.

The Preciousness of Children to God

Children are a gift from God; they are his reward.

—Psalm 127:3, TLB

"Beware that you don't look down upon a single one of these little children. For I tell you that in heaven their angels have constant access to my Father."

—Matthew 18:10, TLB

Once when some mothers were bringing even their babies to Jesus to bless them, the disciples shooed them away, telling them not to bother him.

But when Jesus saw what was happening he was very much displeased with his disciples and said to them, "Let the children come to me, and do not hinder them, for the kingdom of God belongs to such as these. I tell you as seriously as I know how that anyone who refuses to come to God like a little child will never be allowed into his kingdom."

Then he took the children into his arms and placed his hands on their heads and he blessed them.

—Luke 18:15–17, adapted

The Wonder of a Life Created by God

I knew you before you were formed within your mother's womb; before you were born I sanctified you and appointed you as my spokesman to the world.

—Jeremiah 1:5, TLB

You made all the delicate, inner parts of my body, and knit them together in my mother's womb. Thank you for making me so wonderfully complex! It is amazing to think about. Your workmanship is marvelous—and how well I know it. You were there while I was being formed in utter seclusion! You saw me before I was born and scheduled each day of my life before I began to breathe. Every day was recorded in your Book!

—Psalm 139:13–16, TLB

The Pain of Losing a Child

Then Nathan returned to his home. And the Lord made Bathsheba's baby deathly sick. David begged him to spare the child, and went without food and lay all night before the Lord on the bare earth. The leaders of the nation pleaded with him to get up and eat with them, but he refused. Then, on the seventh day, the baby died. David's aides were afraid to tell him.

"He was so broken up about the baby being sick," they said, "what will he do to himself when we tell him the child is dead?"

But when David saw them whispering, he realized what had happened.

"Is the baby dead?" he asked.

"Yes," they replied, "he is." Then David got off the ground, washed himself, brushed his hair, changed his clothes, and went into the Tabernacle and worshiped the Lord. Then he returned to the palace and ate. His aides were amazed.

David replied, "I fasted and wept while the child was alive, for I said, 'Perhaps the Lord will be gracious to me and let the child live.' But why should I fast when he is dead? Can I bring him back again? I shall go to him, but he shall not return to me."

Then David comforted Bath-sheba; and when he slept with her, she conceived and gave birth to a son and named him Solomon. And the Lord loved the baby, and sent congratulations and blessings through Nathan the prophet. David nicknamed the baby Jedidiah (meaning, "Beloved of Jehovah") because of the Lord's interest.

—2 Samuel 12:15–25, TLB

Scripture with Introductory and Transitional Comments

Though _____'s death came rather suddenly, it perhaps was not totally unexpected to her/him. As her/his family shared some of their last conversations with her/him, hindsight suggests that somehow she/he seemed to know death was not far away, and she/he needed to say good-bye to the family she/he loved so dearly.

For people of faith, death is a final farewell before going on to a whole new life, one that does not know the limits of aging or sickness. _____ is enjoying that new life even now; only her/his shell, which she/he no longer needs, remains with us here. The Bible talks about discarding our limited, physical body.

For we know that if the earthly tent which is our house is torn down, we have a building from God, a house not made with hands, eternal in the heavens.

—2 Corinthians 5:1

In that new body "they shall hunger no more, neither thirst anymore; neither shall the sun beat down on them, nor any heat; for the Lamb in the center of the throne shall be their shepherd, and shall guide them to springs of the water of life; and God shall wipe every tear from their eyes."

—Revelation 7:16–17

_____ trusted in that Good Shepherd during this life, and now Christ has faithfully carried her/him on into that new life, according to his words:

Jesus said, "I am the resurrection and the life; he who believes in Me shall live even if he dies, and everyone who lives and believes in Me shall never die."

—John 11:25–26

May we too as her/his friends and loved ones, find comfort and direction from the Holy Scriptures, and particularly from this great passage, Psalm 23, _____'s favorite, as recorded in her/his personal choice of The Living Bible paraphrase:

Because the Lord is my Shepherd, I have everything I need!

He lets me rest in the meadow grass and leads me beside the quiet streams. He restores my failing health. He helps me do what honors him the most.

Even when walking through the dark valley of death I will not be afraid, for you are close beside me, guarding, guiding all the way.

You provide delicious food for me in the presence of my enemies. You have welcomed me as your guest; blessings overflow!

Your goodness and unfailing kindness shall be with me all of my life, and afterwards I will live with you forever in your home.

—Psalm 23, TLB

_____ is now enjoying God's home, because she/he prepared in this life by making her/his peace with God. May we do the same, that one day we too will meet her/him there, in God's home.

———*eo*———

Scripture Medley and Corresponding Prayer

As we stand in the valley of the shadow of death, we draw comfort and strength from the Scriptures, to replace our fear. Both _____ (deceased) and _____ (spouse) enjoyed reading the Psalms in particular. Hear now this medley of Scriptures, drawn from the Psalms. Notice the honesty of feeling with which the psalmist approaches God.

> My God, my God, why hast Thou forsaken me?
> Far from my deliverance are the words of my groanings.
> O my God, I cry by day, but Thou dost not answer;
> And by night, but I have no rest.
> Yet Thou art holy,
> O Thou who art enthroned upon the praises of Israel.
> In Thee our fathers trusted;
> They trusted, and Thou didst deliver them.
> To Thee they cried out, and were delivered;
> In Thee they trusted,
>   and were not disappointed....

Thou art He who didst bring me forth
      from the womb;
Thou didst make me trust when upon my
      mother's breasts.
Upon Thee I was cast from birth;
Thou hast been my God from my mother's womb.
                —Psalm 22:1–5,9–10

I waited patiently for the LORD;
And He inclined to me, and heard my cry.
He brought me up out of the pit of destruction,
      out of the miry clay;
And He set my feet upon a rock making my
      footsteps firm.
And He put a new song in my mouth,
      a song of praise to our God;
Many will see and fear,
      and will trust in the Lord....

Thou, O Lord, wilt not withhold Thy compassion
      from me;
Thy lovingkindness and Thy truth will continually
      preserve me.
                —Psalm 40:1–3,11

God is our refuge and strength,
A very present help in trouble.
Therefore we will not fear,
      though the earth should change,
And though the mountains slip into the
      heart of the sea;
Though its waters roar and foam,
Though the mountains quake at its swelling pride....

"Cease striving and know that I am God;
I will be exalted among the nations,
      I will be exalted in the earth."
The LORD of hosts is with us;
The God of Jacob is our stronghold.
               —Psalm 46:1–3,10–11

Why are you in despair, O my soul?
And why have you become disturbed within me?
Hope in God, for I shall again praise Him
For the help of His presence.
O my God, my soul is in despair within me;
Therefore I remember Thee from the
        land of the Jordan,
And the peaks of Hermon, from Mount Mizar.
Deep calls to deep at the sound of Thy waterfalls;
All Thy breakers and Thy waves have rolled over me.
The LORD will command His lovingkindness
        in the daytime;
And His song will be with me in the night,
A prayer to the God of my life.
               —Psalm 42:5–8

The LORD is my shepherd,
I shall not want.
He makes me lie down in green pastures;
He leads me beside quiet waters.
He restores my soul;
He guides me in the paths of righteousness
For His name's sake.
Even though I walk through the valley of the
        shadow of death,
I fear no evil; for Thou art with me;

Thy rod and Thy staff, they comfort me.
Thou dost prepare a table before me in the presence
      of my enemies;
Thou hast anointed my head with oil;
My cup overflows.
Surely goodness and lovingkindness will follow me
      all the days of my life,
And I will dwell in the house of the Lord forever.
                              —Psalm 23

Thank you, God, for the honesty and relevance of your Word. Just as the psalmist, we experience so many conflicting emotions when we look at loss and death. We are reminded of our own frailness—that our bodies do wear out. We recognize that life really is a precious gift from you. Some of us here have been granted an extension in this life, and for this we are deeply grateful. For _____ (name) it was time to leave this life. Thank you for receiving her/him to glory. Thank you that one day we too will go to her/him, though she/he cannot return to us. May we find comfort and hope from your Word as we grieve our loss. Thank you for being our Good Shepherd through life and death. Amen.

Transition to the Eulogy

We are going to take a few moments now to share our memories of _____'s life. I will begin with the eulogy printed in your bulletin, then a tribute written by _____'s family, and then I'll give you an opportunity to share some of your precious memories of _____ .

What are some of the special memories you have of _____?

Special Note on Eulogies

Since eulogies are usually compiled by the funeral home with family input and are specific to the individual's life history, no examples are given here.

Tributes also tend to be very specific to the deceased. An example is given here to show how a tribute differs from a eulogy. Working with the family to compose a tribute becomes a form of ministry and healing in and of itself.

Example of a Tribute

Grandma _____, as everyone called her, was a special and caring lady. We could tell many stories of the witty woman who stole everyone's heart.

Grandma _____'s "open-door" policy made it easy for anyone to feel free to drop in at anytime. The grandkids especially enjoyed visiting Grandma's house. She always had time to listen to them over coffee or a soda, and they knew they would leave her house with a new joke and a smile.

Unlike most grandmas, she always had the latest variety of cookies or chips. No sooner was she out of the driveway for a family outing than, with a mischievous grin, she would pull out some great junk food snack for everyone. Grandma was a kid at heart.

Grandma _____ was very active. As all her friends know, she loved to play Bingo and cards. If she wasn't doing that, she could be found with knitting needles clicking away in her hands. She was at peace when she knitted, and since she rarely, if ever, kept anything for herself, we knew that a perfect sweater, afghan, mittens, or whatever came to her mind, would be made a gift from her to one of us. She gave more than she ever received.

Grandma's endearing qualities were countless, but one of her most appreciated was her ability to be open to anything. She tried everything, from climbing into her grandson's eighteen-wheeler, to riding her son's motorbike. She shared enthusiasm whenever someone bought something new or tried something different. Grandma _____ was very receptive of everyone. She accepted people the way they were and welcomed them to share their life with her. We all learned from her simple and loving ways.

A tradition with Grandma that never wavered was Christmas Eve. Invitations were never needed. Christmas Eve was always at Grandma's house. We knew that Grandma's house would be full of people, laughter, presents, and more food than you could ever eat. She made sure that everyone had a present, even if that person was an unexpected but welcomed guest.

Grandma _____ was a very special lady, and as put by one of her grandsons, "She loved us all the same, the same way we loved her. I will always cherish the moments I stopped to chat with her." She will be missed by all of those whose lives she touched.

Pastoral Prayers of Thanksgiving

For Closeness, Community, and Comfort

God, our Father, we thank you for the gift of life and all that makes life precious and worth living. We thank you for choosing to place us in family units, where ties of blood and cords of love draw us close together, especially now in our time of need. Thank you for father love and mother love, for the love of husband, wife, and children.

We thank you, too, for the great friends who have come to stand beside us to strengthen our spirits and enlarge our vision. Life in this community is precious to us, Lord, and today we are conscious that a loved one is no longer part of our community. _____'s (first name) death has served to remind us of how great a gift life really is.

And so we are thankful, God, even in death. We realize that our bodies were not made to last forever. They grow weary and worn out. Thank you that in your design there is provision that when our work is done on this earth and our day is spent, we can be released from these earthly forms, freed from the limitations and weaknesses of the aged human body. Thank you, Lord, that _____ has experienced this release.

Father God, we pray your blessing upon the family and friends of _____ . May each of them be provided with the strength and comfort that is needed to sustain them in this hour of sorrow. May we each look to you in faith and receive your gracious support and direction. Amen.

———

For Justice and Mercy

Our God, we are grateful that every one of us is a concern to you and that you deal righteously and justly with us all. Thank you for the life of _____ and that she/he sought to live life in respect of the worth of others and to express a strong sense of fairness, of right and wrong. Thank you for your great love for _____ and of her/his awareness of that love. While it is not clear to us how she/he responded to that love personally, we commit her/his soul to your just and loving care, for you alone know the heart's intent.

You know also the intent of our heart, O Lord. By your mercy, meet us in our pain and turn us ever closer to your loving, outstretched arms. Hold us tightly, we pray. Amen.

———

For Quality of Life

Thank you, Lord, for the many years of life that you gave to
_____ (name). Thank you for the quality of life you gave
her/him to enjoy throughout these years. Thank you for her/his
_____ (unique, remarkable qualities; e.g., sense of
humor, artistic or musical ability, way with people/children/ani-
mals, etc.), the beautiful person you created her/him to be.

And thank you for the loving family you provided to surround
her/him. Be near to them, God, especially now, for they will keen-
ly miss the presence and prayers of this their dear loved one. May
they retain fond memories of a life that was fulfilling, rich with
meaning and purpose, because it was founded securely in you.
For such a rich heritage we bless you, our loving Lord. Amen.

For Finishing Well

Thank you, God, for granting _____ the gift of ___ years of
life. Each day is indeed a gift from you, and we praise you for
this multitude of gifts you granted her/him.

Thank you too for all the relationships that _____
enjoyed. Many of those special people are gathered here today
to say farewell to this one whom they loved. Some knew
her/him as the beloved matriarch/patriarch/ of the family.
Others knew her/him as Grandma/Grandpa, Aunt/Uncle, or
Mom/Dad. Still others experienced her/him as a coworker, a
neighbor, a friend. Thank you, Lord of relationships, for the rich
ties that bind us to _____ .

Lord, we are grateful for the many years of health and vitality with which you blessed _____ . Thank you for the good
care she/he received to the very end, when her/his health did
begin to fail. Thank you for helping _____ to finish well.

And though we are sad today, O Lord, we are also thankful for the many precious memories with which we are left. These memories will live on, far beyond today, continuing to enrich our lives and the lives with whom we share them. We are indeed richer for having known _____ , and for this we give you praise. Amen.

————◦◦◦————

For Release from Pain

Loving Father, we are touched by the memories of those who have just lost a loved one. Memories are indeed a precious gift. Thank you for the gift of families; thank you for love and friendship. Thank you for the long life and experiences you gave _____ and for how she/he touched our lives, whether as father/mother, husband/wife, brother/sister, grandfather/grandmother, or friend. Thank you for this opportunity to remember and to share those memories.

But, Lord God, we also are experiencing the pain of death and separation. Though we would not wish her/him back to the painful limitations she/he had prior to leaving us, our pain is now real. We will miss her/him. Thank you for meeting us in our grief. Thank you for releasing _____ from his/her pain. Thank you for the healing you will bring through the grief process, healing that will begin to lessen our pain. Thank you for caring loved ones with whom to share this time of sorrow. Thank you for your comforting presence here that brings us hope in the midst of our pain. In Jesus' name. Amen.

————◦◦◦————

For Strength amid Turmoil

This pastoral prayer is intentionally lengthy to encourage mourning family and friends to linger in the presence of God.

Heavenly Father, _____'s death has filled our eyes with tears and our hearts with sorrow. We are distressed at the mysteries of your providence when it does not coincide with what we think is good and right.

As children of your creation, we want so much to say with confidence that all things are fitting together for our good, but we honestly confess that in the present circumstance we find it almost impossible to do.

Only you know how much we would long to have seen _____'s life blossom into full maturity. She/he possessed so much talent in her/his character, so much eagerness to pursue life and all it has to offer. Surely, Lord, you understand the grief, the disappointment, the sense of loss we feel, for you too lost a son in untimely death to this hostile earth.

And so, in spite of the loss and the sorrow that hinder us, we do want to come to you, Lord. We do want to have you share with us as you shared with Mary and Martha at the tomb of Lazarus, to weep with us as you wept with them.

We readily acknowledge here and now, Lord, that though we can often seem to get by on our own strength, at this particular occasion you are the only one sufficient to heal our wounded hearts and wipe the tears from our eyes. We know that you understand that we have not come angrily to toss our grief and disappointment into your face. Rather, we come, as you have invited us, to cast our cares upon you and have you comfort and sustain us in our anguish.

And so, Lord, we come.

We come to thank you, God of life, for the gift of life. And we especially offer our gratitude to you for the life of _____, who has so suddenly departed from our midst. We thank you for her/his _____ years on this earth and for the things in her/his life that prompted family and friends to love her/him. Thank you for the privilege of sharing in her/his life, brief as it was.

God of all comfort, we also come to ask that in your love and tenderness you watch over these loved ones whom _____ leaves behind. We don't have to tell you about the depth of their sorrow, for you already know it, but in the stillness of our own hearts we would ask for them your constant help and comforting presence. Be their keeper during this distressing trial; be the strength of their otherwise fainting hearts; and be the light of their darkened home. We ask that you would help them to pick up the pieces and, in time, build again. Fill their emptiness with peace. Give them courage and strength, sufficient for each hour.

Loving Father, as we walk through this valley of the shadow of death, continue to let us know you are with us! Thank you for the warmth and comfort your presence brings to us. Thank you for caring so deeply for each one of us. Thank you for your strength, even now. Amen.

For Meaning and Purpose in Life

Father God, we praise you for our blessed hope. Thank you that there is so much more to life than simply living a certain span of time here on earth, struggling for our existence, and then finding that it is all over. Thank you for the meaning and purpose you give to life by showing us how life here is but a tiny star in a vast universe when compared with everlasting life. Thank you, too, for the choice you give us in this life that forms the basis of our life beyond the grave. We are so grateful today that we know _____ chose in this life to commit her/his life to you, Father, and that now she/he is in your comforting presence as a result of her/his decision. Now she/he has the peace of mind that she/he always sought, for meaning and purpose are fulfilled as we draw nearer to your presence.

And so, Father, it is not for her/his present state, but our own, that we pray. We are the ones who must continue on, living life without her/him, again finding our own meaning and purpose. We pray especially for _____ *(spouse)* and _____ and _____ *(children by name)* as they seek to pick up the pieces and begin to live again without _____.

We pray for ourselves, that as a church family we might seek to somehow lessen that great void left by a missing life. Help us to be very practical in our love for _____ (spouse) and the children. Remind us in the lonely weeks and months ahead to reach out with that special touch of love that will truly make the difference in helping them cope for that day. And thank you again so much for your ongoing touch of love and comfort daily, moment by moment, to each one of us. In Jesus' name we pray. Amen.

Appropriate Special Music

"How Great Thou Art"
"Ivory Palaces"
"One Day at a Time"
"Precious Lord, Take My Hand"
"Through It All"

Funeral Address Outlines

From Psalm 23

I. Choose and follow the Shepherd.
II. Find in God the guidance, comfort, and strength we need.
III. Plan to meet him at his home when our time comes.

From Psalm 39:4–7

I. Death is a normal part of this earthly life.

II. Death frees us to a heavenly new life.

III. Death reminds us to prepare in the first for the second.

From John 14:1–7

I. Death comes with finality.

II. Death is not the final end, but a new beginning.

III. Jesus is the door beyond death to our new home.

From 1 John 1:1–9

I. Like John, we can know Christ personally.

II. Like John, we can enjoy fellowship with God.

III. Like John, we must make this faith our own.

From 1 John 1:9

I. Reassess our priorities.

II. Make our peace with God.

III. Respond to God's invitation.

    A. If we confess our sins (Agree we are a sinner)

    B. He is faithful and just to forgive us (Believe)

    C. And cleanse us from all unrighteousness (Claim)

Selected Scriptures: Where Is God in This?

I. The emotion of anger.

    A. Exodus 11:10–17

    B. John 11:17–27

II. The emotion of pain.

    A. John 11:28–37

    B. 2 Corinthians 1:3–7

III. The emotion of guilt.

    A. John 3:17–18

    B. Romans 8:1

Benedictions

And now may the LORD bless you, and keep you; the LORD make his face to shine upon you, and be gracious to you; the LORD lift up his countenance upon you, and give you peace.

—Numbers 6:24–26, adapted

And now may the God of hope fill you with all joy and peace in believing, so that by the power of the Holy Spirit you may abound in hope.

—Romans 15:13, adapted

And now may the peace of God, which passes all understanding, keep your heart and mind through Christ Jesus.

—Philippians 4:7, adapted

Now may our Lord Jesus Christ himself and God our Father, who has loved us and given us eternal comfort and good hope by grace, comfort and strengthen your hearts, and help you in every good thing you say and do.

—2 Thessalonians 2:16–17, adapted

The grace of the Lord Jesus Christ be with your spirit.

—Philemon 25, NRSV

And now may the memory of _____ , whom we have loved, linger long to bring us comfort and consolation. May the death of this husband/wife, daughter/son, loved one, and friend draw each of us into a closer partnership with God, that the Lord might minister to us in our grief. And may the God of peace, who raised Jesus Christ from the dead, grant to us the knowledge and assurance of eternal life. Amen.

The Committal Service

Announcements

This is an example of an announcement regarding the committal service and lunch following. Making an announcement is helpful for informing people about which cemetery is being used and for giving them the option, if they feel they are unable to attend this part of the service, of remaining at the church and waiting for the family's return. This is especially important in inclement weather.

You are all invited to the _____ cemetery now for a brief committal service. If you are driving a vehicle, please turn your lights on and follow the funeral coach to the cemetery. If you do not wish to attend this final committal, you are welcome to remain here at the church for the lunch that will follow once the family returns.

Scripture Texts for Committal

Jesus said, "I am the resurrection and the life. Those who believe in me, even though they die, will live, and everyone who lives and believes in me will never die."

—John 11:25–26, NRSV

We know that if the earthly tent which is our house is torn down, we have a building from God, a house not made with hands, eternal in the heavens.

—2 Corinthians 5:1

In that new home, "They shall hunger no more, neither thirst anymore; neither shall the sun beat down on them, nor any heat; for the Lamb in the center of the throne shall be their shepherd, and shall guide them to springs of the water of life; and God shall wipe every tear from their eyes."

—Revelation 7:16–17

Committal Service Remarks

In this spirit of hope, based on these Scriptures, we commit _____'s spirit into the care and keeping of a just and merciful God, and we tenderly commit her/his body back to the earth from which it came, earth to earth, ashes to ashes, dust to dust.

A Committal Prayer

Our Lord, whether we live or die, we know that we are in your compassionate care. Here, then, we commit to your unfailing love the soul of one whom we love. Thank you for the gracious memories and kindly deeds that live on with us. Thank you for the privilege of sharing her/his life. May those whom she/he leaves behind know the comfort, strength, courage, and guidance of your Holy Spirit in the days to come. Through Jesus Christ our Lord. Amen.

Committal Benedictions

An appropriate benediction may be drawn from the list given above. Simply choose a different one than what was used in the church service.

APPENDIXES

Additional
Wedding
& Funeral
Resources

Author's Permission

THE RESOURCES IN THESE appendixes may be photo-copied and kept on file, ready at a moment's notice. Alternatively, the text is available online at www.judsonpress.com. Adapt the forms and guidelines to your situation and download or reproduce them as needed. Included in these resources are:

Appendix A: Wedding Interview Guide. Use this form when a couple meets with you for the first time regarding getting married. Adapt this form to fit your needs. Use it as your guide for the interview rather than having them fill it out.

Appendix B: Procedural Guidance and Information Sheet. Most churches have a wedding policy. This sheet may be used as a comparison or to begin such a policy for your church. It is also a helpful way to suggest the going rates of remuneration for services rendered.

Appendix C: Church Wedding Application Form. Use this to confirm the booking of the church and of additional services. This form also requests the information needed to complete paperwork required of the minister by the Canadian government.

Appendix D: Wedding Order of Worship Planning Sheet. This checklist is to be used with the couple for planning out the details of the wedding ceremony itself.

Appendix E: Wedding Service Format Checklist. This planning form is also to be used for personalizing the wedding plans.

Appendix F: Wedding Usher Job Description. This form is provided to help orient the ushers to their job. Since these people are chosen by the bride and groom, they may never have ushered before. They may also be from another town and be unfamiliar with the church facility. Thus it is very important to orient them to their task during the rehearsal so that a positive tone is set as people arrive for the wedding.

Appendix G: Additional Samples of Wedding Vows. This sheet could be given to couples as they make their choice of vows or as they write their own. These vows have been adapted from minister's manuals as listed.

Appendix H: Funeral Planning Checklist. This checklist is a helpful organizational tool when emotional trauma surrounding a death makes it difficult to focus and plan appropriately. Keep it readily available.

Appendix I: General Funeral Details Worksheet. This tool is perhaps best used first at the funeral home in discussing the service and other details with the funeral director.

Appendix J: Funeral Service Elements Form. Use this form to plan the details of the funeral service with a family.

May you find these practical tools helpful in your ministry.

APPENDIX A

Wedding Interview Guide

1. What are some of the reasons you desire to marry each other?

2. What things are important to you in choosing a church wedding?

3. Where do you each see yourselves as being in your spiritual pilgrimage of getting to know God?

4. How important is God to you, and what part will God have in your marriage?

5. What will be your ongoing commitment to God and this church following the wedding?

6. Are you both willing to attend _____ sessions of premarital counseling?

Review: Premarital counseling options
Legal requirements
Procedural guidance and information sheet
Church wedding application form

APPENDIX B

Procedural Guidance and Information Sheet

The pastor(s) will guide and assist you in making your wedding a truly high and holy occasion in your lives.

Marriage in _____ Church is considered to be "instituted of God, regulated by his commandments, blessed by our Lord Jesus Christ, to be held in honor among all people." The marriage ceremony is performed only in the context of divine worship in this church. Your wedding will mean more to you, your families, and friends when careful consideration is given to the sacred aspects of this holy occasion.

Scheduling
Please plan in advance for the use of the sanctuary. The minister will help you with your personal wishes concerning the wedding based on availability. A time for counseling should be arranged and the date for the wedding set as early in the wedding planning stage as possible.

Officiating
The pastor (or associate pastor) of the church will officiate at all weddings. If another clergy member is desired to conduct the ceremony, please provide that person's name and telephone number so that he or she may be contacted by this office.

The officiating minister(s) will meet with the wedding party for a wedding rehearsal to explain all procedures. Please have the entire wedding party, including the ushers, present promptly at the prearranged time.

The marriage license should be in the minister's possession one week before the wedding.

Music

Music is an important part of a wedding ceremony. Since weddings in our sanctuary are in the context of worship, music selections need to be appropriate. The choices to be made should be discussed with the pastor during planning of the wedding service. If you are uncertain about appropriate selections, he can offer traditional and more contemporary favorites. The pastor may also provide names of vocalists or musicians as needed.

Decorations

The church suggests tasteful simplicity in decorations. Please do not use nails, thumbtacks, or glues that may stain to attach decorations to the seats, windows and sills, doors, railings, and other surfaces. Please use dripless candles in the candelabra, as wax is difficult to remove from the flooring. Be certain to make arrangements in advance if you will need access to the sanctuary to decorate prior to the day of the ceremony.

Photographers

Please instruct your photographer that flash pictures are not permissible in the sanctuary from the end of the processional until the recessional. Nonflash pictures may be taken discreetly if they do not distract from the worship service. The presence of the photographer him/herself should also be as unobtrusive as possible during the ceremony.

Wedding Contributions

When the bride or groom or one of their parents is an active member of the church, the following contributions are suggested:

Use of sanctuary	no charge
Custodian	$25
Organist	$50 (includes rehearsal and wedding)
Soloist	$25

When neither the couple nor their parents are members of this church, the following contributions are suggested:

Use of sanctuary	$25
Custodian	$25
Organist	$50 (includes rehearsal and wedding)
Soloist	$25
Minister	$75

The bride and groom are required to sign the Church Wedding Application Form, agreeing that they understand and will comply with the foregoing guidelines. Reservations for the church will be considered firm when the signed confirmation form is returned to the church office.

APPENDIX C

Church Wedding Application Form

1. Date of wedding *(month, day, year)*: _____

2. Groom's SSN: _____
    (Canada—social insurance number)

3. Bride's SSN: _____
    (Canada—social insurance number)

Groom

4. Surname _____

    All given names _____

    _____

5. Marital status: ☐ never married, widowed, or divorced

    ☐ divorced: _____

    If divorced, give date when the divorce was finalized (U.S.), or date of decree absolute of divorce proceedings (Canadian)

6. Religious affiliation: _____

7. Birth date *(month, day, year)*: _____

8. Age on wedding day: _____

9. City, town, state/province or country of birth: _____

    _____

10. Current address *(before marriage)*

    Street: _____

City: _____

State/Province: _____

Postal/Zip Code: _____

11. Residence telephone: _____

Business telephone: _____

12. Father's name: _____

13. Birthplace of father *(Canada)*: _____

_____

14. Mother's name: _____

Maiden name *(Canada)*: _____

15. Birthplace of mother *(Canada)*: _____

_____

Bride

16. Surname _____

All given names _____

_____

17. Marital status: ☐ never married, widowed, or divorced

☐ divorced: _____

If divorced, give date when the divorce was finalized (U.S.), or date of decree absolute of divorce proceedings (Canadian)

18. Religious affiliation: _____

19. Birth date *(month, day, year)*: _____

20. Age on wedding day: _____

21. City, town, state/province or country of birth: _____

_____

22. Current address *(before marriage)*

Street: _____

City: _____

State/Province: _____

Postal/Zip Code: _____

23. Residence telephone: _____

Business telephone: _____

24. Father's name: _____

25. Birthplace of father *(Canada)*: _____

_____

26. Mother's name: _____

Maiden name *(Canada)*: _____

27. Birthplace of mother *(Canada)*: _____

_____

General Information

28. Officiating minister: _____

29. Suitable premarital counseling times: _____

30. Address after wedding

Street: _____

City: _____

State/Province: _____

Postal/Zip Code: _____

We have carefully read the Procedural Guidance and Information Sheet for weddings at _____ (name of church) and will comply with the established guidelines.

Signature of the bride: _____

Date: _____

Signature of the groom: _____

Date: _____

APPENDIX D

Wedding Order of Worship Planning Sheet

Usual elements
(Check the elements you want in your wedding.)

_____ ☐ Prelude

_____ ☐ Seating of the Mothers

_____ ☐ Candle Lighting

_____ ☐ Processional

_____ ☐ Introduction of Ceremony

_____ ☐ Opening Prayer

_____ ☐ Giving of the Bride

_____ ☐ Hymn(s)

_____ ☐ Scripture Reading

_____ ☐ Pastoral Counsel (Message)

_____ ☐ Special Music

_____ ☐ Vows

_____ ☐ Exchange of Rings

_____ ☐ Declaration of Marriage

_____ ☐ Prayer of Dedication

_____ ☐ Unity Candle Ceremony

_____ ☐ Signing of the Register (Canada only)

_____ ☐ Introduction of Newlywed Couple

_____ ☐ Recessional

_____ ☐ Postlude

_____ ☐ (Receiving Line)

_____ ☐ (Reception)

Special additions (Optional)

_____ ☐ Communion

_____ ☐ Special Acknowledgments or Tributes (e.g., moment of silence for a deceased parent, gift of rose to mother or mother figure)

_____ ☐ Alternate Special Music

_____ ☐ Involvement of Children

_____ ☐ Other: _____

_____

_____

Selected order

The elements above are listed in the typical order, but this is your wedding. Number them in the order you would like them to occur.

APPENDIX E

Wedding Service Format Checklist

Personnel

☐ Maid / Matron of Honor: _____

☐ Best Man: _____

☐ Number of attendants: _____

Names: _____

_____

_____

☐ Flower girl(s)? If yes, name(s): _____

_____

☐ Ring bearer(s)? If yes, name(s): _____

_____

☐ Candle lighters? If yes, names: _____

_____

☐ Ushers? If yes, names: _____

_____

_____

☐ Pianist: _____

☐ Organist: _____

☐ Other instrumentalist? _____

☐ Vocalist? _____

Service Music

☐ Processional: _____

☐ Recessional: _____

☐ Special music

    Number of selections: _____

☐ Hymns: _____

Style of service
Entrance Options: Bridal Party

☐ Men from the front, women down aisle *(traditional)*

☐ As couples down aisle

☐ Other: _____

Entrance Options: Bride

☐ Bride on father's left arm *(traditional)*

☐ Bride with both parents down aisle

☐ Other: _____

Processional Options

☐ hesitation step *(back foot up to join front foot, then lead out again)*

☐ regular steps *(walk slowly)*

Vows

☐ traditional

☐ chosen *(offer copies of contemporary options)*

☐ original *(personalized and created by bride and groom)*

Lighting of the Unity Candle

☐ tapers lit before ceremony

    ☐ by candle lighters

    ☐ by mothers/parents

    ☐ by *(names):* _____

☐ tapers lit during ceremony by bride and groom

☐ special table on platform

☐ on altar

☐ accompanied by music

    If so, song and musician: _____

☐ leave individual tapers lit

☐ extinguish individual tapers

Signing of the Register
(Canadian services only)

☐ special table on platform, as public part of the ceremony
(Some couples like a special tablecloth, such as Grandma's, on this table.)

☐ side office *(Couple and witnesses leave with pastor during special music to sign the legal documents; then all return to complete the ceremony.)*

☐ other: _____

_____

Allowance of Flash Pictures during the Ceremony

☐ yes   ☐ no

☐ if no, brief announcement by minister with promise to pose afterwards?

Publication of Service Order

☐ Formal bulletin for congregation.
If so, composed and printed by whom?

_____

☐ Informal order held by pastor and pianist/organist only

Times
Wedding rehearsal:

Date: _____   Time: _____

If not at ceremony site, specify location:

_____

Wedding ceremony:

Date: _____   Time: _____

Reception:

Location: _____

Date: _____ Time: _____

Married Name Desired

(i.e., How do you wish to be introduced to the congregation at the conclusion of the ceremony?)

☐ **Traditional:** Mr. and Mrs. husband's full name
(e.g., Mr. and Mrs. Harry Smith)

☐ **Shared Last Name:** Mr. and Mrs. husband and wife's first names, shared last name *(e.g., Mr. and Mrs. Harry and Jane Smith, or Mr. and Mrs. Harry and Jane Jones-Smith)*

☐ **Hyphenated Last Name (wife only):** Mr. and Mrs. husband's full name, wife's first name and hyphenated last name *(e.g., Mr. and Mrs. Harry Smith and Jane Jones-Smith)*

☐ **Retain Own Names:** Mr. and Mrs. husband's name, wife's name *(e.g., Mr. and Mrs. Harry Smith and Jane Jones)*

☐ **Omit "Mr. and Mrs." in any of above options**

☐ **Other:** _____

APPENDIX F

Wedding Usher Job Description

Instructions to Ushers

1. Arrive at least one half-hour prior to the wedding ceremony.

2. Check lighting, ventilation, and location of the guest register, restrooms, and other facilities that guests may ask about. Confirm that everything is in place.

3. Seat guests who arrive early as they are ready.

4. You are the host. Smile and welcome people. Give directions as needed.

5. Offer your right arm to escort women to their seats. Men will simply follow you.

6. Leave the front pew empty in case someone from the wedding party suddenly needs to be seated.

7. Immediate family should be seated near the front of the sanctuary. Reserve the second row for the parents and grandparents of the couple. Siblings may be seated in the third and fourth rows as needed.

8. Tradition dictates that the bride's family and friends be seated on the left side of the aisle; seat the groom's family and friends on the right side of the aisle. Seat friends of the couple on the side that seems slowest to fill.

9. Escort grandparents and then parents to their designated seats, usually just before the wedding ceremony is scheduled to begin. (As an alternative, the mothers may be escorted by the groom or by a male relative in the bridal party.)

APPENDIX G

Additional Samples of Wedding Vows

From the Baptist Tradition 1
The Charge
Pastor: _____ *(groom),* will you have _____ *(bride)* to be your wedded wife, to live together in the covenant of faith, hope, and love according to the intention of God for your lives together in Jesus Christ? Will you listen to her inmost thoughts, be considerate and tender in your care of her, and stand by her faithfully in sickness and in health, and, preferring her above all others, accept full responsibility for her every necessity as long as you both shall live?

Groom: I will

Pastor: _____ *(bride),* will you have _____ *(groom)* to be your wedded husband, to live together in the covenant of faith, hope, and love according to the intention of God for your lives together in Jesus Christ? Will you listen to his inmost thoughts, be considerate and helpful in your support of him, and stand by him faithfully in sickness and in health, and, preferring him above all others, accept full responsibility for his every necessity as long as you both shall live?

Bride: I will

Vows
I, _____ *(groom),* take you, _____ *(bride),* to be my wedded wife, to have and to hold from this day forward, for better, for worse; for richer, for poorer; in sickness and in health; to love and to understand till death shall part us, according to the design of God in creation, and I commit myself completely to you.

I, _____ *(bride),* take you, _____ *(groom),* to

be my wedded husband, to have and to hold from this day forward, for better, for worse; for richer, for poorer; in sickness and in health; to love and to understand till death shall part us, according to the design of God in creation, and I commit myself completely to you.[1]

From the Baptist Tradition 2
The Charge

Having freely and deliberately and prayerfully chosen each other as partners for life, will you please unite your right hands.

_____ (groom), you are now entering a relationship with many privileges but also many obligations. The woman you love is about to become your wife. In no way could she so tell of her love for you as by her willingness to turn from home and loved ones and friends, true and tried, to make her home with you. Your joys will be her joys and your sorrows her sorrows. Your people will be her people and your God her God.

_____ (bride), you too are entering into a relationship with many privileges and obligations. The man you love is about to become your husband. He tells the world not only of his willingness but of his express desire to turn from all others and to you for all of life ahead. Your love will be his inspiration and your prayers his tower of strength.

And now, here in the presence of God and these witnesses, do you take each other as husband and wife, agreeing to love each other devotedly and to promote each other's happiness until this union into which you are entering is dissolved by death? Do you promise?

Response, together: I promise.

Exchange of Rings

Take the ring, _____ (groom), and place it upon

_____'s *(bride's)* finger, and, as you do, repeat to her after me these words:

With this ring I thee wed, and all my worldly goods I thee endow. In sickness and in health, in poverty or in wealth, till death do us part.

Take the ring, _____ *(bride),* and place it upon _____'s *(groom's)* finger, and, as you do, repeat to him after me these words:

With this ring I thee wed, and all my worldly goods I thee endow. In sickness and in health, in poverty or in wealth, till death do us part.[2]

From the Episcopal Tradition
The Charge
Pastor: _____ *(groom),* will you have this woman to be your wife, to live together in a holy marriage? Will you love her, comfort her, honor and keep her, in sickness and in health, and forsaking all others, be faithful to her as long as you both shall live?
Groom: I will by God's help.
Pastor: _____ *(bride),* will you have this man to be your husband, to live together in a holy marriage? Will you love him, comfort him, honor and keep him, in sickness and in health, and forsaking all others, be faithful to him as long as you both shall live?
Bride: I will by God's help.
Pastor: (to wedding party and congregation) Will you who witness these vows do all in your power to support and uphold this marriage in the years ahead?
Response: We will by God's help.

Vows
I, _____ *(groom),* take you _____ *(bride)* to be my wife, to have and to hold from this day forward, for better, for

worse; for richer, for poorer; in sickness and in health; to love and to cherish until we are parted by death. This is my solemn vow.

I, _____ *(bride)*, take you _____ *(groom)* to be my husband, to have and to hold from this day forward, for better, for worse; for richer for poorer; in sickness and in health; to love and to cherish until we are parted by death. This is my solemn vow.[3]

From the Lutheran Tradition
The Charge
Pastor: _____ *(groom)* and _____ *(bride)*, if it is your intention to share with each other your laughter and your tears and all that the years will bring, by your promises bind yourselves now to each other as husband and wife.

Vows
Groom: I take you _____ *(bride)* to be my wife from this day forward, to join with you and share all that is to come; and, with the help of God, I promise to be faithful to you as he gives us life together.
Bride: I take you _____ *(groom)* to be my husband from this day forward, to join with you and share all that is to come; and, with the help of God, I promise to be faithful to you as he gives us life together.[4]

An Abbreviated Marriage Ceremony
The Introduction
This rite of marriage in which you now come to be united is the first and oldest rite of humankind. Marriage is our foretaste of paradise, given in the wisdom of God to soothe the troubles and increase the joys of our earthly life. This it will do for you, if you purpose in your hearts to beautify and sweeten it by your tender devotions, your mindfulness in little things, your patience

and sacrifice of self to each other. Coming in full love to the threshold of a new life together, I commend to you these spiritual ministries as the way to lasting happiness.

The Charge
Pastor: Will you _____ , *(groom)* take this woman to be your wedded wife, promising to keep, cherish, and defend her and to be her faithful and true husband so long as you both shall live?
Groom: I will.
Pastor: Will you _____ , *(bride)* take this man to be your wedded husband, promising to adhere unalterably to him in all life's changes and to be his loving and true wife till death divide you?
Bride: I will.

Vows and Exchange of Rings
Groom: I, _____, take thee, _____, to be my wedded wife, to have and to hold from this day forward, for better, for worse, for richer for poorer, in sickness and in health, to love and to cherish until death us do part.
Bride: I, _____, take thee, _____, to be my wedded husband, to have and to hold from this day forward, for better, for worse, for richer for poorer, in sickness and in health, to love and to cherish until death us do part.[5]

Alternate Wedding Promises
_____ , I take you to be my wife/husband from this time onward, to join with you and to share all that is to come, to give and to receive, to speak and to listen, to inspire and to respond, and in all circumstances of our life together to be loyal to you with my whole life and with all my being.

I take you _____ , to be my wife/husband. I promise before God and these witnesses to be your faithful husband (wife), to share with you in plenty and in want, in joy and in sorrow, in sickness and in health, to forgive and strengthen you and to join with you so that together we may serve God and others as long as we both shall live.

I take you, _____ , to be my wife/husband, and these things I promise you: I will be faithful to you and honest with you; I will respect, trust, help, and care for you; I will share my life with you; I will forgive you as we have been forgiven; and I will try with you better to understand ourselves, the world, and God through the best and the worst of what is to come as long as we live.[6]

I, _____, receive you, _____, as a gift from God, to be my lifelong companion. I will love you through laughter and tears, through health and sickness, in plenty and in want, at work and at play. I will love you constantly and with the deepest loyalty. I will prayerfully seek your joy and happiness throughout our lives. Amen.[7]

Notes

1. *Adapted from Perry H. Biddle Jr.,* Abingdon Marriage Manual *(Nashville: Abingdon, 1974), 126–33.*
2. *Adapted from Samuel Ward Hutton,* Minister's Marriage Manual *(Grand Rapids: Baker Books, 1968), 55–57.*
3. *Adapted from Biddle, 133–49.*
4. *Ibid., 150–63.*
5. *Adapted from Hutton, 42–45.*
6. *Adapted from Biddle,* Abingdon Marriage Manual, *172–73.*
7. *Adapted from Jesse C. Middendorf,* The Church Rituals Handbook *(Kansas City, Mo.: Beacon Hill Press, 1997), 80–81.*

APPENDIX H

Funeral Planning Checklist
(For the Pastor and the Bereaved Family)

Time of funeral: _____

    Location: _____

Interment following? _____

    Location: _____

Funeral home involved: _____

Lunch following at the church? ☐ Yes ☐ No

    If yes, who will prepare and serve food? _____

_____

Will there be a viewing of the body? ☐ Yes ☐ No

    If yes, ☐ family viewing ☐ open viewing

    Dates and times? _____

Names of pallbearers: _____

_____

_____

_____

Who will prepare the bulletin, including the biographical sketch

of the deceased? _____

Who would you like to participate in the service?

☐ pianist; name: _____

☐ soloist; name:_____

☐ ushers; names: _____

_____

_____

☐ someone to read a tribute or deliver eulogy; name:

_____

☐ other: _____

_____

Favorite hymns or Scripture readings of the deceased:

_____

_____

_____

Would you like to establish a memorial to be given toward, in lieu of, or in addition to, flowers? If so, provide relevant information:

_____

_____

_____

_____

APPENDIX I

General Funeral Details Worksheet
(For the Pastor and Funeral Home Director)

Although many funeral homes now take care of most of the following arrangements, it is advisable to check these details with the funeral home and/or the family of the deceased.

Has a grave plot been selected? ☐ Yes ☐ No

Is a family plot desired? ☐ Yes ☐ No

Which cemetery is being used? _____

_____

_____

Has grave digging been arranged? ☐ Yes ☐ No

Have arrangements been made for a headstone (if desired)?

☐ Yes ☐ No

Has a casket been chosen? ☐ Yes ☐ No

If cremation is chosen, will there be a viewing first?

☐ Yes ☐ No

If yes, are there rental caskets available? ☐ Yes ☐ No

What is to be done with the deceased's ashes?

_____

_____

In the case of a memorial service, closed-casket funeral, or a cremation without a viewing, is there a framed recent portrait of the deceased available for display during the service?

☐ Yes   ☐ No

Is additional transportation of the body needed?   ☐ Yes   ☐ No

Who is preparing the bulletin? _____

_____

_____

Who is placing the announcements of the funeral on the radio

and in the newspaper? _____

_____

_____

Note: The funeral home will need the deceased's social security (U.S.) or social insurance (Canada) number.

APPENDIX J

Funeral Service Elements Form

The following elements are usually included in a funeral. Use and adapt them to fit the current need.

Funeral Service

☐ Prelude

☐ Processional

☐ Opening remarks

☐ Prayer of invocation

☐ Hymn

☐ Scripture readings

☐ Eulogy

☐ Tribute

☐ Prayer of thanksgiving for deceased's life

☐ Special music

☐ Funeral address

☐ Hymn

☐ Benediction

☐ Postlude and processional

Committal service

☐ Scriptures

☐ Remarks

☐ Prayer

☐ Benediction

Annotated Bibliography

Recommended Reading on Ministerial Ethics

Hughes, Philip E. *Christian Ethics in Secular Society.* Grand Rapids: Baker Books, 1983.

> A general introduction to the theology of Christian ethics, this book is written for Christians in general rather than specifically for ministers. It lays a helpful theoretical foundation.

Trull, Joe E., and James E. Carter. *Ministerial Ethics: Being a Good Minister in a Not-So-Good World.* Nashville: Broadman and Holman, 1993.

> Written specifically for ministers, this book covers the moral choices and responsibilities of pastors in all their personal relationships, from personal integrity to standing in the community. Several sample codes of ethics are provided, including those for different staff positions.

Recommended Reading on Grief Counseling

Doka, Kenneth J., ed. *Living with Grief After Sudden Loss: Suicide, Homicide, Accident, Heart Attack, Stroke.* Bristol, Pa.: Taylor & Francis, 1996.

Developed from the teleconference of health-care professionals sponsored by the Hospice Foundation. Has a helpful annotated resource list on traumatic loss.

Kuenning, Delores. *Helping People through Grief*. Minneapolis: Bethany House, 1987.

Has a number of sensitive chapters on helping parents grieve the loss of a child, from a variety of causes, ranging from murder to miscarriage. Concludes with a helpful summary of dos and don'ts for caregivers.

Manning, Doug. *Don't Take My Grief Away: What to Do When You Lose a Loved One*. San Francisco: Harper & Row, 1984.

Written for individuals who have just encountered the death of a loved one, it explains how to plan a funeral. It then discusses how to understand death, grief, changes, and recovery. A main thesis is how to treat grief as a friend rather than an enemy and use it to grow back to health.

Meyer, Charles. *Surviving Death: A Practical Guide to Caring for the Dying and Bereaved*. Rev. ed. Mystic, Conn.: Twenty-Third Publications, 1991.

Presents various views of death and dying, gives suggestions for helping families make ethical choices concerning life support, outlines challenges for the church to respond to the needs of the dying, and considers several theological misconceptions regarding death.

Reinsmith, A. M. Brady. *Surviving Grief: 30 Questions and Answers for a Time of Loss*. Valley Forge, Pa.: Judson Press, 2001.

A small volume that answers some of the honest and difficult questions that bereaved persons ask as they work through the grieving process. Helpful for the survivors themselves as well as for pastoral and other caregivers. Includes a list of recommended reading and support groups.

Williams, Donna R., and Joann Sturzl. *Grief Ministry: Helping Others Mourn.* San Jose: Resource Publications, 1990.

> Focuses on ministering to those in grief, whether the loss is death or some other significant event like divorce. Provides tools to help caregivers overcome fears of death, equipping them for coming alongside those in grief, whether those persons be adults or children.

Other Helpful Minister Manuals

Biddle, Perry H., Jr. *Abingdon Marriage Manual.* Nashville: Abingdon Press, 1974.

> Provides ideas for ministry to the couple before and after the wedding, as well as for the wedding itself. Written for a broad spectrum of denominations and includes a typical wedding service for United Methodist, Baptist, Episcopal, Lutheran, and Presbyterian churches. Includes a section on state marriage laws.

Biddle, Perry H., Jr. *Abingdon Funeral Manual.* Nashville: Abingdon Press, 1976.

> Companion volume to the *Abingdon Marriage Manual.* Similarly ecumenical in focus.

Cram, William, ed. *A Manual for Worship and Service: Prepared for Canadian Baptist Churches.* The Baptist Federation of Canada: All-Canada Baptist Publications, 1976.

> My personal favorite, because it helped me through my early years of ministry "firsts." This volume includes weddings, funerals, and a variety of other special services of the church. A revised version was published in 1984.

Hutton, Samuel Ward. *Minister's Marriage Manual.* Grand Rapids: Baker Books, 1968.

> Covers a variety of details, from marriage service elements to wedding etiquette. Includes a wide variety of

wedding services, including Episcopal, Lutheran, Methodist, Presbyterian, Catholic, and Jewish.

Hutton, Samuel Ward. *Minister's Funeral Manual.* Grand Rapids: Baker Books, 1968.

Companion volume to the *Minister's Marriage Manual.* Similarly ecumenical in focus.